Advance Praise for *Gender Physics*

"Betty-Ann's insight into the gender dynamics of business examines an essential question: What does it take to create something extraordinary? Having helped artists give birth to hundreds of great songs and multiplatinum records, it took decades of trial and error to learn what Betty-Ann teaches us in *Gender Physics*. In an entertaining and engaging way, her stories succinctly illustrate how the natural integration of Masculine and Feminine Energies contributes to achieving success on a truly broad scale. *Gender Physics* challenges an urgent and contemporary dialogue, especially relevant within the context of today's contentious political climate. It makes sense that the traditional world could well benefit from this work."

—**Tim Collins**, Music Industry Entrepreneur, best known for orchestrating the comeback of Aerosmith, AKA America's Rolling Stones

"I, and many of my executive coaching clients, often feel like aliens because the person we want to be doesn't fit with what we are told we should be. We leave meetings wondering if we acted incorrectly, as if there were exact norms to follow. I am so grateful for the engaging way *Gender Physics* shows how we can freely express ourselves and be successful on our own terms. It is a must-read for everyone looking to be courageously authentic at work and in life."

—**Dr. Marcia Reynolds**, Author of *Outsmart Your Brain; Wander Woman: How High-Achieving Women Find Contentment and Direction; and The Discomfort Zone: How Leaders Turn Difficult Conversations into Breakthroughs*

"*Gender Physics* is a book that deserves serious attention by both women and men. Its thesis is that our best selves are a blending of what we think of as feminine and masculine. Indeed, this book aligns with my thinking that if women want to move forward in their careers, they need to transcend the traditional 'female' patterns of behaviour and adopt attributes we think of as 'male.' And if men want to move ahead, they need to add on qualities we think of as 'female.' This visionary book shows both sexes how to realize their full potential, and it does so with a strong and captivating narrative."

—**Judith Humphrey**, Author of *Taking the Stage: How Women Can Speak Up, Stand Out, and Succeed*

"Modern organizations depend on a vibrant, diverse talent pool for success. Understanding how to create conditions that enable employees to bring their full selves to the workplace improves engagement, which leads to optimum productivity. Betty-Ann's study of gender physics offers practical insights into gender-based behavioural tendencies that are highly applicable to the workplace. For talent specialists, Betty-Ann's narrative is filled with learnings that will inform leadership and performance assessments. *Gender Physics* is a thought-provoking, and often humorous, journey intended to unshackle unconscious biases that often undermine organizational — and social — excellence. Applying Betty-Ann's lessons will improve an employer's brand and an organization's competitive advantage."

—**Stephen Brown**, Director, Talent Acquisition, Ontario Public Service

"*Gender Physics* is a game-changer. Betty-Ann expertly explores balancing energies through a fascinating exploration of a range of variables, rooted in her nearly 30 years of work as a leading executive. Deftly making references to film, politics, current events, television, and culture, Betty-Ann brings to life the notion of gender as a social construct and provides tangible advice on how we can each harness our innate Masculine and Feminine Energies to live authentically, be the truest expression of our highest selves, and make our dreams come true. She takes us through a process of introspection and self-reflection, guided by her own experiences and supplemented by exercises that allow us to immediately understand the relevance of these lessons in our own lives. A natural and generous storyteller, Betty-Ann is brave, bold, vulnerable, and honest in *Gender Physics*, sharing some of her greatest successes and biggest challenges with a view to showing us that we are not alone. Her book inspired me to look within and evaluate my own life to see how I can become more of who I truly am. At its core, *Gender Physics* is a call to action, reminding us to be the stars of our own films, the narrators of our stories, the vibrant, unique sparks in our own lives and the world. Because, as Dorothy learns in *The Wizard of Oz* and as Betty-Ann shows us through her trailblazing work, we have 'always had the power.'"

—**Prasanna Ranganathan**, Lawyer, Speaker, Associate Producer, Writer, and Social Media Correspondent

Gender Physics

Unlock the *Energy* You Never Knew You Had to Get the *Results* You Want

Betty-Ann Heggie

Member of Canada's Top 100 Most Powerful Women Hall of Fame

Library and Archives Canada Cataloguing in Publication data available upon request.

Published by Cremini Books, an imprint of The Harvest Commission

ISBN 978-0-9950821-3-7 (paperback)
ISBN 978-0-9950821-4-4 (ebook)

Printed in Canada

TO ORDER: orders@creminibooks.com

Book producer & managing editor: Tracy Bordian
Design (cover & interior) & layout: Rob Scanlan/First Image
Cover graphic: Andrei Dobrescu
Copy editor: Eleanor Gasparik
Proofreaders: Karen Alliston and Joel Gladstone
Indexer: Karen Hunter

For more information, visit **www.bettyannheggie.com**

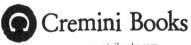

www.creminibooks.com

To my mother,

who loved reading,
thought the greatest gift was a book,
and shared that enjoyment with her children
and grandchildren. She would have relished seeing
this book come to fruition but, sadly, didn't live
that long. Still, she unwittingly provided the basis.

When my grade four teacher decided I was
too spirited for my gender and tried to put me in
the good-little-girl feminine box,
my mom wouldn't stand for it.

She marched into the school and told the
teacher in no uncertain terms that her job
was to teach me science, math, and spelling
but to leave my personality alone.

She demanded that I be given the freedom
to be myself and develop my individuality.

Thanks, Mom—this one's for you!

Contents

Chapter One

Breaking Gender Boxes

It was the early 1990s and my go-to fashion accessory was a necklace with a big fake pearl that dangled around my neck on a long gold-colored chain. I considered it a fashion coup, but the guys in my office saw it differently, suggesting it explained my 'ballsy' behavior—I mean, there *had* to be an explanation as to why this new, inexperienced investor relations person wasn't acting like a 'girl.' Rather than being cautious and demure, I was prone to action, fearlessly picking up the phone to book a meeting with Peter Lynch, the famous investor who wrote *One Up on Wall Street*. As our company lawyer often said, "Look out if you disagree with her—it's like walking into a buzz saw."

These male colleagues expected women to show them some deference, to clean up the coffee cups after management meetings, laugh at their jokes, and support their opinions. They certainly didn't expect a woman to challenge them and question their traditional way of conducting business. If I had had the proper body parts they probably would have accepted my behavior and secretly admired my gutsiness, considering me a 'real man.' Yet, because I was female, it upset the status quo, making them uncomfortable and suspicious of me. Ultimately, they concluded that the explanation for my 'masculine' behavior had to be that necklace. It made me one of them. I wore that 'big ball' daily and told my colleagues that it came from the last guy who disagreed with me. "Beware," I laughingly said. "Do you want yours hanging around my neck?"

During nearly three decades of working in a masculine environment, I had to be an independent, self-sufficient risk-taker who wasn't afraid to protect my territory and assertively express strong positions. In short, I lived my life outside traditional gender stereotypes. It served me well, but because it wasn't conventional, it caused me to think a lot about the constraints of our gender conditioning. Gender is such a large part of our personal identity, and yet it often prevents us from living freely as individuals. The first word that nine out of ten people will use when asked to describe themselves (or others) is "man" or "woman." "Boy or girl?" is the first thing we ask when a baby is born, before placing a pink or blue yoke around their neck. With that yoke comes an expectation of how that person should look or act or to whom they should be attracted.

> Gender is such a large part of our personal identity, and yet it often prevents us from living freely as individuals

Then, attached to archaic gender views, we line up and take sides to make our side right and the other wrong. Unfortunately, seeing the opposite sex as separate from us can deteriorate into name-calling, prejudice, discrimination, and even violence. This not only hurts others but also stunts our personal growth and limits couples, companies, communities, and countries.

Each of us is a unique medley of characteristics, so trying to fit into gender boxes usually means stifling our unique talents—the things that make us truly special. If we aren't being real, we can't pursue our dreams. Furthermore, acting out a facade of someone other than who we really are is depleting and diminishing. It is like the 80/20 rule in business, which says that you get 80 percent of your business from 20 percent of your customers. If you are being who you were meant to be, you'll get 80 percent of your results from 20 percent of your effort. You'll have more energy and you'll avoid burnout.

These antiqued gender boxes, established centuries ago, make it difficult for men and women to adapt to modern family living. Men no longer need to be the sole breadwinner and can instead equally partner with women—sharing child-care and financial responsibilities. Gender boxes also stifle effective parenting. Girls are discouraged from testing boundaries to take advantage of opportunities while boys are dissuaded from exercising the giving and listening skills often considered feminine, which are increasingly required in our multifarious world.

By giving up limiting stereotypes, both energies present in us can emerge and work together

As adults joining the workforce, women who have been conditioned to avoid risk are reluctant to voice their thoughts and opinions. Not only is their advancement thwarted but also their companies miss out on valuable input. Men who have been conditioned to avoid feeling their feelings have difficulty relating to the feelings of others, often becoming leaders who can't empathize with their constituencies.

Gender boxes also develop two distinct types of leaders: women who are expected to be collaborative, caring relationship-builders, able to bring people to a consensus, and men who are expected to be independent, action-oriented risk-takers, able to assertively close the big deal. This is to our detriment. Business in today's multifaceted economy requires increasingly diverse leaders whose management techniques enable them to move agendas forward while still taking care of their stakeholders.

Our business success is hampered as well. Astute leaders know that hiring the right talent for the position and developing that talent is integral to a company's productivity and bottom-line results. Yet, while we work to bring out the best in others, we often stifle our own skills and talents by adopting only the attributes assigned to our gender. Talent management requires that we align our natural attributes (and those of our employees) with the right projects at the right time for optimal performance. Gender conditioning limits this. It is time for some reevaluation.

It doesn't have to be this way, as none of us is either/or; rather, each of us is both. Because we see ourselves as one gender or the other, we use only half of the actions and options available to us, and we often end up stuck in a repetitive pattern, unaware of the full range of our choices. The alternative is to use our Feminine Energy to get to know ourselves and build relationships with others and our Masculine Energy to lead the way and reach our goals.

These two energies are present in every one of us regardless of our biology, and we don't have to go on a massive search to find them. It is as simple as giving up limiting gender stereotypes to allow our Masculine and Feminine Energies the freedom to emerge and work together. This is the road toward balance.

Humans are naturally attracted to balance, so individuals who access both energies are bestowed with the magical (and influential) quality of 'presence.' These are the people you are intuitively attracted to on the street and who stand out in a crowded room. You might say they have 'it'—the panache, the charisma, the special quality of standing apart from the throng. It is presence that not only makes us want to be near them but also makes us want to help them reach their goals. Not surprisingly, this makes presence a huge benefit in business.

Additionally, balancing our energies keeps us from overusing our strengths. Consider the high-performing production manager whose vigilance makes them exceptionally efficient at delivering quality products at competitive costs. If they dial up their focus on the goal to the extreme, they can become overly controlling and run the risk that employee relationships will suffer. Too much of a good thing is definitely a bad thing, and it can be avoided by using both energies in the optimal proportions.

> Using both energies and shifting between them prevents our strengths from becoming weaknesses

It is time for us to leave behind duality—to move beyond 'he' and 'she' and be complete human beings. By pushing past 'the right way or the wrong way' mentality, we'll reduce divisiveness and find common ground. Recognizing that we are different expressions of the same will help us bridge the gap with those in our communities who hold disparate views. Hopefully by doing our part at a local level, it will spread to polarized leaders around the globe, as people and systems that are 'out of balance' invariably topple.

Releasing our gender conditioning does not mean that we must take off our kid gloves or give up our man-cards, but it does mean integrating both Feminine and Masculine Energies into our consciousness. That will better enable us to:

- become more rounded individuals and whole human beings
- be more aware of our preference while understanding others' points of view
- develop the magnetic characteristic of presence
- keep our strengths from becoming weaknesses
- be perceived as confident and caring leaders

The dynamic interdependent relationship between Feminine and Masculine Energies is what I call Gender Physics—and it is an idea whose time has arrived. We all know that with only one wing you will never fly. Your two wings already exist, but until you spread them both, you'll never know how high, fast, or far you can soar.

Gender Physics is the dynamic relationship between Feminine and Masculine Energies

This is at the heart of what I have devoted my adult life to: the need for society to give up its limiting attachment to gender and let each of us be who we truly are. By unlocking the energy we never knew we had, we can get the results we want. Furthermore, with this better awareness and acceptance of one another as individuals, rather than as either a man or a woman, we can all get down to business!

Important Note: The theory and concepts in this book come from my business experience and subsequent research. They are demonstrated through my personal stories and also through movies, as visual storytelling is so experiential. Throughout the book I encourage you to be an individual, so please approach the content that way as well. You may wish to roll up your sleeves and get immediately into how Gender Physics works in the Variable chapters (3 to 8). Or you may be someone who likes to learn as you go: if so, feel free to dive right into the experiments in Chapter 9. Of course, you can always follow the content as it unfolds in the order presented.

Wise Leaders Use Both Gender Energies

I was fortunate to work with a man who deftly demonstrated the advantages of using both gender energies, and the experience had a long-lasting effect on me. It was 1987 and the world potash market was completely out of balance. There was too much supply and not enough demand. New production was being opened while customers ceased to buy. Thus, market prices fell, profits were nonexistent, and companies were bleeding red.

Our owners, the Government of Saskatchewan, did what many companies do when they are losing money: they replaced the top echelon. Our CEO was fired and a new one was brought in. They went not only outside of our company to find him but also outside of the country. Our new CEO was an American southerner who talked funny—at least to us. Essentially, to the people of Saskatchewan, he was a complete outsider. He was also a man with a military background—very hierarchical and teeming with Masculine Energy. I could have called him a "walking talking Viagra tablet."

Our new leader walked in and, without preamble, assessed our numbers, determined that the company needed to cut back production, and announced the closure of a mine. People were livid.

"How dare an outsider come in and close a mine!" they exclaimed. "This is our mine, our natural resources, and our jobs. What right does he have to take them away?"

Soon after this unpopular announcement, a letter to the editor appeared in the local newspaper. Amongst other allegations, the author contemptuously declared that the new CEO couldn't "manage his way out of a pay toilet." After the letter's publication, it was our CEO's turn to be livid, and the rest of us scrambled for cover. He demanded an immediate investigation, and the executives (me included) were tasked with hunting down the culprit who had penned the defamatory missive. After some digging, it was discovered that the author had used a fabricated name. However, the phone number provided was real, and it was quickly traced to the home of an hourly paid employee. But, as it turned out, it wasn't the employee who had written the letter—it was his wife.

So, what did our new CEO do? Well, clearly he could have pounced on their mistake, publicly humiliated the woman, or even fired her husband. As mentioned, he was a man rife with Masculine Energy and someone who could have easily dialed it up to the extreme, choosing retribution as his action. He did none of these things and instead tapped into his (previously unseen by us) Feminine Energy. He invited the letter writer to meet him on neutral territory, a coffee shop in the Sheraton Hotel. The woman arrived, shaking like a leaf, terrified of the fate that awaited her.

Surprisingly, our CEO refrained from raising his voice—in fact, he didn't talk … at all. Rather, he sat listening quietly (Feminine Energy) as she lamented the friends and neighbors she would lose when they relocated to Calgary because of the company layoffs.

When our CEO finally did speak, his voice was thick with … empathy, another Feminine Energy attribute. He spoke of how his own father had been an hourly paid worker and of how he understood, firsthand, the pain and frustration of continually being uprooted. He reminisced about his seven-year-old self: forced to move to a new location, leaving behind his best friend Billy, a boy he never saw again. From his heart, he talked about his feelings. He and this wife and mother made an emotional connection that day. They found common ground.

> Our CEO demonstrated the value of the Feminine Energy trait of empathy

By the time they parted, the aggrieved woman had become his new best friend. Later, she even added him to her Christmas-card list. Whatever animosity she had held toward him had evaporated over a few cups of coffee. By accessing his Feminine Energy, he made an advocate out of an adversary. She became one of his greatest supporters, telling her husband, her husband's coworkers, and their wives that, under the circumstances, our CEO was doing the best that he could for the company. She described it as cancer by saying, "You don't like having to do it, but sometimes you have to cut out part to keep the being alive."

Our new CEO had used Masculine Energy to make the tough decision to close the mine, and again to find the person who had written the letter. Had he allowed Masculine Energy to dominate and sought revenge, he would have escalated the situation and therefore the problems of the company, harming our reputation and relationships beyond repair.

On the other hand, had he used only Feminine Energy, he never would have found the conviction to close the mine in the first place or acted to find the author. He could have become a frustrated, unproductive victim. But he didn't get stuck in either energy—instead, he expertly utilized and balanced both energies, demonstrating wisdom.

Wise leaders are known for choosing the best action for every situation, and that ability comes from accessing both Masculine and Feminine Energies.

Giving Up Gender

Movie protagonists who overcome great obstacles also demonstrate the dynamic use of these two interdependent energies. Consider the 2016 sci-fi hit film *Arrival*, which casts Amy Adams as Louise Banks, a linguistics expert who must translate sounds emanating from heptapods (seven-limbed aliens) who have landed on Earth. Recruited by the American government, Banks is tasked with finding out what they are doing here. Unarmed, she accesses her Masculine Energy and bravely removes her hazmat protection. Then through facial expression, the inflection in her voice, and listening, she uses her Feminine Energy to communicate with the aliens, thus preventing war with the nations on Earth. Demonstrating both courage and caring, Adams convincingly offers a heartrending example of the importance of incorporating both energies into our repertoire.

To develop this 'full circle of ourselves,' we have to break the boxes and give ourselves permission to live outside society's gender expectations. When we accept that our behavior and the way we do things are not givens, we'll come to the realization that gender is a social construct and we can open ourselves to the many benefits of Gender Physics.

After working almost exclusively with men all my life, I have concluded that there are more variations between people within the gender than there are differences between the genders themselves. The same guys who would, in the safety of my office, passionately discuss concerns for their children, felt compelled to act ruthlessly and convey no doubt when discussing the company's strategy with fellow male executives in the boardroom. They were like musical instruments tuning themselves to blend in with the opinions held by others.

Occasions where my male counterparts and I dealt with situations identically occurred so routinely that I came to believe we are not hardwired dissimilarly. Our real differences came from the established models imposed upon us at birth that we then felt we had to live up to. We are a product of our environment, as it is very difficult to separate ourselves from our culture.

> Our labels at birth influence our self-perception and establish the models that we then live up to

Important Note: The attributes of each gender and the advantages of using both have been discussed and researched in many different forms throughout history. While the notion is not new, what is new is acknowledging, acquiring, and focusing on the skills needed to achieve a better balance within ourselves as we get down to business. A quick review of some of the evidence can be found in Appendix 1.

Expressing Our Individuality

Each of us comprises a medley of characteristics that makes us unique. No matter our gender, we could be a restless explorer or a dreamy poet, quietly withdrawn or the life of the party. We may love to sing heavy metal while playing air guitar or to read philosophical novels while sipping red wine in the bathtub. Each of us is a little bit of this and a little bit of that, combining different characteristics to different degrees.

We all want to be recognized and valued by our colleagues for our individuality, but our effort to fit in means that we wedge ourselves into traditional molds rather than expressing the unique magic in ourselves. We lose so much by supporting the status quo rather than expressing our special gifts and talents and experiencing life as we want it.

By practicing Gender Physics we can embrace the things that make us different and freely express ourselves using the characteristics typically considered the domain of the opposite gender. We can let go of any guilt or uneasiness if we are a girl who wants to spend her weekend rebuilding a car engine or a boy who wants peace and solitude to write poetry.

Your Energy Flows Like Water

Using both your energies is like drawing water from the tap. To quench your thirst, you turn on the cold water. To take a relaxing bath, you turn on the hot water. This is no different from choosing Feminine or Masculine Energy for different situations, audiences, or venues. Just like water temperature, there are times when one energy works better than the other. You don't want the water to get so hot that you burn yourself, so you adjust by adding some cold. Adjusting your energies works the same way. Add a little of its opposite to find exactly the right combination to suit your needs. Also remember: whether the water is hot or cold, it is still H_2O flowing from the faucet. It is the same with you. You can bring forth your personal energy by using Feminine or Masculine Energy, and it is still *you being you.*

Let's Be Humans, Not Genders

The challenge is to step back and accept that people are just people, rather than thinking of them separately as male or female. Sandra Bullock eloquently expressed this at the Toronto International Film Festival (TIFF) in September 2015 while discussing her role in the film *Our Brand Is Crisis.* Bullock told the audience that her part had originally been written for a man. George Clooney was supposed to play it but was too busy to accept the role.

When Bullock read the script, she loved the dynamic part and blazed forward, asking the producers to make the lead female rather than male. They agreed to the gender swap and, other than changing the character's name, hardly had to tweak the role at all. Imagine, she mused, if Hollywood became an ocean of great roles, not written specifically for either men or women but written instead for humans.

Shortly after hearing Bullock's comments, I read that Stephenie Meyer, author of the wildly successful Twilight series, had swapped genders of the main characters in her newest novel. Meyer had committed to writing extra content for Twilight's tenth anniversary, but finding herself short of time, decided to rewrite the opening chapters of her original book by throwing gender aside.

It made no difference if the human personality was male and the vampire female, she concluded. She also used the rewrite as an opportunity to discount disapproval regarding the character of Bella. She had been criticized for being consumed by a love interest, but the rewrite proved that infatuation isn't necessarily a 'girl' thing. Meyer found that writing outside of the gender box was not only fun but also "really fast and easy." She went on to estimate that only 5 percent of the character traits needed any kind of rewriting.

That we are one and the same was reaffirmed once again by Patty Jenkins, director of 2017's blockbuster film *Wonder Woman*, when she said: "I wasn't directing a woman. I was directing a hero."

> **Important Note:** Generalizations are fraught with peril, but they can be useful in helping us make sense of the world. For example, artists, both male and female, are generally characterized as being emotional and sensitive, more apt to march to the beat of their own drum. Business people are often characterized as being hard and cold, concerned more about money than people. Yet there are many artists who are practical and many caring executives. When I speak about gender, please know that I do not mean all men or all women, as they are certainly not monolithic groups. Furthermore, when I speak of Masculine Energy, I am not referring only to men; nor does Feminine Energy refer only to women.

Presence Comes from Using Both Energies

People who balance both energies are like magnets. Balance is attractive, as demonstrated by the golden mean in geometry. This perfectly balanced ratio is seen in such famous architectural creations as the Great Pyramids and the Parthenon, as well as in the paintings of Renaissance artists Leonardo da Vinci and Michelangelo. People find these balanced and harmonious works reassuring, stimulating, and enormously satisfying. They are attracted to them in the same way that they are attracted to those who have presence.

Presence would fetch a high price could it be bottled and sold, but for many, acquiring this precious commodity proves difficult. Yet, like the golden mean, it comes alive when others subliminally recognize the beauty of you as a balanced human being.

I first recognized these dynamics years ago while conducting a research project for a university class on social networks. It was fascinating to see the way that everyone wanted to work with a select few individuals. When I looked more closely at the attributes of these magnetic people, I found that they were not only confident and capable but also cooperative, encouraging, and validating. Others benefited from their expertise, yet found working alongside them pleasant and amiable.

Later, during my tenure with Xerox Canada, one of my responsibilities as a salesperson was surveying customers to ensure product satisfaction. While we strove to deliver good-quality copies to every customer, I noticed that there were distinct differences in how those copies were perceived. If a repair person cared about their customer, the customer not only liked them but also would accept substandard copies. In fact, they would rate their copies as excellent! Conversely, even top-notch copies would be rated below average if those doing the repairs didn't act as if they cared about the customer.

Both situations drove home that if you care about others, it can positively influence their perception of your ability. Such is the significance of Feminine Energy. In our production-oriented society, we have tended to undervalue the benefits of Feminine Energy, but this is a reminder, once again, that Masculine Energy isn't appreciated without it.

By balancing Feminine Energy caring and connection with the confidence and competence of Masculine Energy, people have the magnetic gift of presence. When both characteristics are present, the sum total is enhanced.

Bringing Beliefs in Line with Biology

Biologists used to believe that sex determination happened at birth, that our brains dictated the differences in our behavior. Now, evidence has led them to conclude that our brain is plastic, that it has the amazing ability to constantly develop and change throughout our lives. New pathways are constantly created based on our environment and where we put our attention. Thus, our brains alter and adapt to external influences, which affects our thoughts and expectations about being male or female. This in turn affects our behavior.

The Tel Aviv University research study "Sex Beyond the Genitalia: The Human Brain Mosaic" was published in December 2015. It concluded that "brains are brains" and they aren't male or female. The authors of the study analyzed MRIs of more than 1,400 human brains and concluded that brains differ in individual ways, just as our appearances, retinas, personalities, and fingerprints are uniquely our own, but they do not have specialized features that flag them as one gender or the other. Furthermore, the researchers deduced that brains with features that are consistently at one end of the maleness-femaleness continuum are rare. Rather, most brains are composed of a montage of features.

There are those who would argue that the differences in the genders are due to the hormone testosterone, but recent studies show that behavior influences hormones more than hormones influence behavior. Academic psychologist Cordelia Fine points out in her book *Testosterone Rex* that many studies demonstrate how testosterone increases when people experience stress or achieve positions of power. Conversely, testosterone decreases when people care for infants.

While science is disproving physiological gender differences, we also see the irrelevance of gender playing out in the public forum. For example, beginning in 2014, UK Facebook users could choose from more than seventy-one gender choices. Only one year later, Facebook announced that its US users didn't have to respond to a preconceived set of gender boxes; they could completely customize their gender identity. I applaud these expanded options to reflect people's individuality.

The late artist, musician, film star, and fashion icon David Bowie led the way by defying all categories. When he first appeared on the scene, many surmised that he was gay, then he was widely touted as being bisexual, and finally, after he had married twice and fathered two children, heterosexual. For this he was called a chameleon. If Bowie had allowed himself to be pigeonholed into a traditional gender role, he might never have created, and left us with, such a unique and game-changing legacy. Today, he is recognized as one of the great musical innovators of our time. And the fact that he freely roamed the gender spectrum was, I believe, one source of his genius.

While men have always been expected to exhibit Masculine Energy and women Feminine Energy, we now know that there is no inherent physical reason why this should be. By bringing our beliefs in line with our biology, we'll be free as individuals to express ourselves with a mix of gender characteristics.

Archetypes Help Us Learn the Ropes

We often say, "Oh yes, I know the type," when talking about people, and we are referring to archetypes. Humans have been categorizing behavior and patterns of energy into archetypes for centuries. It helps us learn the ropes.

There are ancient archetypes and more current ones, yet throughout history, we have consistently sorted people and inanimate objects into Feminine and Masculine. Interestingly, the attributes assigned are very similar around the world. For example, in every culture and throughout history, we see the sun as the hard-driving, get-up-and-go Masculine and the moon as the mysterious, relax-and-let-go Feminine. Day is different from night, and we can easily describe the differences. Day is not superior to night, nor is night superior to day, and so it is with Masculine and Feminine.

> *Important Note:* I capitalize Masculine Energy and Feminine Energy throughout this book because I use the terms to denote social as opposed to physical constructs. When I refer to Masculine and Feminine or Masculine and Feminine Energies, I am referring not to biological genders or the physical attributes that make a man or a woman, but to behavioral archetypes. Also, note that unless I am describing someone specific, I don't use "he" or "she"; instead, I use the gender-neutral "they" or "them."

Feminine and Masculine Archetypes

An example of a Feminine archetype would be the caring nanny Mary Poppins, who answered the ad for a kinder, sweeter nanny placed by the lonely forlorn children Jane and Michael Banks. Julie Andrews played that part, and she showed us another Feminine archetype as Maria in *The Sound of Music*. In that role, she brought playful abandon to motherless children who, until her arrival, had been ordered about by their militaristic, whistle-blowing father.

An archetype of a Masculine male would be the Scottish soldier and landowner Jamie Fraser from the popular television series *Outlander*. Strong and courageous, he takes on anyone who poses a threat to his clan, friends, and family, regardless of what it costs him personally. Other confident, adventuresome Masculine archetypes out to save the world would be Harrison Ford in the Indiana Jones franchise and Sean Connery, the original James Bond.

There is nothing wrong with having archetypes. The problems occur when archetypes become stereotypes and prescribe how we should be in the world. This stifles our individuality. As singer/songwriter Miley Cyrus says, "Being a girl isn't what I hate, it's the box I get put into."

Archetypes Can Become Stereotypes

A good example of the way that we stereotype was documented in research conducted by Lera Boroditsky, a professor at Stanford University. While English isn't a language that classifies nouns as masculine or feminine, many languages do. Boroditsky took an image of a bridge, showed it to people in Germany, and asked them to describe it. In German, a bridge is feminine. Reflecting feminine gender stereotypes, German people said the bridge was elegant, peaceful, pretty, and slender.

Then Boroditsky showed the same image of the same bridge to people in Spain, where the word for bridge is masculine. They described the bridge as being big, strong, sturdy, and towering. Clearly, we have strong expectations of things that we deem to be either masculine or feminine.

Another study, from the University of Illinois at Urbana–Champaign and entitled "Female Hurricanes Are Deadlier Than Male Hurricanes," showed that hurricanes with female names generally result in three times more fatalities than those with male names. Why? The reason had nothing to do with the power of the storm and everything to do with people's reactions to the storm warning. They knuckle down and prepare for storms with male names because their stereotypical expectation is that the storm will be stronger and more violent. Thus, they are more prone to evacuate for Hurricane Victor than for Hurricane Victoria.

Categorization encourages the belief that if one side is right then the other is wrong

It's clear that we don't see our world holistically but rather dualistically, in two parts. These strong beliefs in duality began in the Middle Ages around 1,500 years ago and have not abated. At one time this brought us closer together by helping us better understand our world, but now it widens the gaps amongst us. Today, everything in our lives is compared and labeled: good or bad, happy or sad, beautiful or ugly, rich or poor. Unfortunately, categorization encourages the belief that if one side is right then the other is wrong. Instead, we need to develop the awareness that things that appear divergent and opposite are really different ways to convey the whole.

This thought was poignantly demonstrated in the 2015 Oscar-winning animated film *Inside Out*, which explored the emotions of joy, fear, anger, disgust, and sadness in a prepubescent girl named Riley. In the control center of her mind, the emotions coexist in homeostasis until her father takes a job in another city and she is suddenly uprooted. Before the move, joy is Riley's predominant emotion, but as she navigates her new life, negative emotions begin to vie for position. Ultimately, Riley realizes that although experiencing sadness is painful, without it, she cannot feel happiness—one frames the other.

Our binary beliefs are reinforced by systemic socialization, pulling men toward the use of Masculine Energy attributes and women toward Feminine Energy ones. Below is a chart that breaks down some typical ways in which girls and boys have been conditioned in society.

Boys are socialized to be:	Girls are socialized to be:
Curious	Demure
Always on the go	Onlookers sitting pretty and passive
Focused on the goal	A source of dreamy creativity
Externally driven	Polite and of service to others
Constantly testing boundaries	Cautious and risk averse
Independent	Nurturing
More interested in playing games than forming relationships	Ready to stop games if feelings are hurt

Stereotypes Create Unconscious Bias

Gendered behavior is not inherent. It comes from stereotypical socialization that started at birth and is then programmed into the software of our subconscious. Mostly, our subconscious is an obliging, industrious little helper that has our best interests at heart. Truly wanting to be of assistance, it acquires and assimilates information as efficiently and expediently as possible. Then it uses that information as the basis for making thousands of mundane decisions each day, such as what's for lunch.

Conclusions drawn by our subconscious can manipulate our behavior in areas such as what we buy, how we work, and our style of parenting without us even realizing it. John Bargh gives examples of this in his book *Before You Know It: The Unconscious Reasons We Do What We Do*. For example, his experiments showed that students who did a test unscrambling the word *elderly* subsequently walked down the corridor more slowly, and that test participants holding a hot (versus cold) drink rated a stranger as "having a 'warmer' personality."

Bargh also researches how stimuli affect free will, as our subconscious can be dogmatic and make decisions that are contrary to what we consciously want. These hidden beliefs create unconscious bias. Being aware of how bias affects us is important because we have conscious access to only a small percentage of our brain. It's not that we are hiding our prejudices. Most often, we simply aren't aware that we have them.

Due to unconscious bias, those who don't adhere to traditionally expected gender behaviors are often treated with suspicion. This prods each of us into Gender Pull, which means that men present themselves using Masculine Energy and women with Feminine Energy. Gender Pull is like the physics theory of gravitational pull. The latter describes why we keep our place on the planet, and the former describes why we keep to the place denoted by our gender.

The Importance of Releasing Gender Pull

Women are conditioned to be careful, yet society says that they must step forward and confidently take risks to be considered a leader. Many believe that 'getting the job done' can only be accomplished by those who exhibit Masculine Energy, so releasing their Gender Pull is important for women in business.

A 2014 study from Michigan State University published in *Psychology of Women Quarterly* questioned whether women should "man up" when applying for a job in a male-dominated field. And in fact, it showed that women have a better chance if they describe themselves with Masculine attributes such as assertive, independent, and achievement-oriented. Those who emphasized traits most often considered Feminine, such as warmth, support-iveness, and nurturing, were unlikely to get hired.

Stanford Graduate School of Business had similar findings. They followed 132 women graduates over eight years; the research results were published in the *Journal of Occupational and Organizational Psychology*. They concluded that women who displayed Masculine traits in business and could dial these characteristics up and down, depending on the situation, received more promotions. Of interest: their ability to monitor themselves and avoid backlash meant that they surpassed not only other women but men as well!

To be hired and promoted, women must use Masculine Energy; yet they must simultaneously cloak those attributes within the folds of Feminine Energy communal behavior in order to not be labeled with the "B" word. It's a tricky balancing act and can only be accomplished by using Gender Physics.

Societal conditioning also restricts men's performance. I first became aware of this in my Gender Physics workshops when asking for examples of men who possess Masculine Energy. Male participants would typically answer "Putin or Trump" and cite character- istics such as being domineering and all-powerful, and having a winner-takes- all mentality. Though personifying this out-of-balance Masculinity is not who most young men are, or even who they want to be, it is often their perception of what society expects of them. Unfortunately, this can cause their careers to stagnate.

Fear of rejection motivates men and women to express the attributes of their gender

The Future of Work, published by *The New York Times Magazine* in 2017, advised men to give up hard hats, saying that the American workforce—once defined by making things—is now largely driven by serving others. In order to do this, men need to access their Feminine Energy. In fact, Columbia Business School encourages students to develop a more sensitive leadership style by having them practice interpreting body language and facial expressions to improve their emotional intelligence. "We never explicitly say, 'Develop your feminine side,' but it's clear that's what we're advocating," associate professor Jamie Ladge told *The Atlantic* magazine in an article entitled "The End of Men."

Understanding Gender Pull and using this knowledge will help not only individuals reach their objectives but also com- panies get better results. For example, if they want to improve collaboration, adding women to teams will most often make it easier to reach consensus, as they have been socialized to set up flat organizations where everyone will be heard. Conversely, if they want something done expediently, it often helps to add men, as they are trained to establish clear steps from top to bottom and to delineate roles clearly.

Gender Pull Limited Me

Like others, I have been a victim of the limiting hazards of Gender Pull during my career. There was a time when I stayed in my Feminine Energy and used too much caution when, instead, I should have confidently crossed over into my Masculine Energy and asserted myself.

One day when working in my office, the head of the mergers and acquisitions department came to my door. I enjoyed this fellow's company and, whenever he came by, I welcomed the break. On this day, though, I could tell by his demeanor that he had something serious to discuss. "We need to talk," he said. I pulled away from my computer and joined him at the round table next to the corner window.

Known for his no-nonsense, businesslike manner, he got straight to the point. Our company had just completed the acquisition of some potash assets in the Middle East. The ink was still drying on the paper, and he wanted me to know that included in the deal was the provision that our company send over a manager to run the operation.

"I think that you would be perfect for the job, Betty-Ann. It involves diplomacy, good communication skills, and marketing ability."

The position was all about building relationships, and my proven track record in investor relations and sales made me his number-one candidate. Part of me was flattered by his assessment of my attributes, but my mind flew to those that I knew I lacked, namely, production experience.

As if reading my mind, he said, "Don't worry about production management—that's our area of least concern. We know that we can't get all the requisite skills in one person, but you have the most important ones, and they're already good operators." With that, he answered my unspoken misgivings.

Feminine Energy is risk averse

Perhaps he thought that my skills were enough, but what about the production people? Would they be happy and supportive of someone outside the engineering fraternity? Again, he was way ahead of me.

"I've discussed it with both the COO and HR, and all of us agree that you're the best candidate. We've already recommended you to the CEO."

The entire management team had been unanimous about my recommendation. It seemed that it had a good chance of going ahead—if I wanted it.

My stomach fluttered. It was an exciting opportunity. I was an avid traveler and, combined with my love for foreign cultures, the idea of living and working in another country was more than a little appealing. I was also acutely aware that international experience offered a fast track for advancement. International experience, coupled with overseeing an operation, would make me a much more valuable commodity within the company. Finally! I had been doing the same job with the company for many years, somewhat stagnating for someone who enjoyed learning and the challenge of growth. Smiling, I told him that

I would discuss it with my husband. But we both knew that he had me hook, line, and sinker.

The next day, the CEO came by my office. He strode in purposefully and sat in the chair closest to the door, which was a nonverbal signal in itself. I had not been advised that he wanted to speak with me, nor invited to sit equally at the table with him.

"I hear that the guys have talked to you about going to the Middle East," he said. I nodded affirmatively, but before I could respond, he added, "You don't want that job. It is the same level as a mine manager, and you are a senior vice president." It was a statement, not a question; he had made up his mind.

> Those with Masculine Energy have no trouble asserting themselves

"Oh, but yes, I do," I responded with as much conviction as I could muster. "The position will utilize my current strengths and give me the opportunity to acquire new ones."

He resisted all my arguments and stated that the company needed me where I was. Mostly, he reiterated that the job was beneath me. It became obvious that, for whatever reason, the CEO didn't want me in this position.

"You like your current job, don't you?"

It was a loaded question, with perhaps the hint of a veiled threat. I knew that not everything would go as planned in this new venture. There would be hiccups, and without the support of the CEO, my margin for error would be minimal. Feminine Energy does not like to take risks. Suddenly all my fears and uncertainty rose to the fore: Would my husband be happy in a foreign land where I'd be putting in long hours? What would we do for a social life when we left all our friends behind? Would my young adult children who were away at university feel abandoned? Did I want to earn my credibility in a male-dominated environment all over again, and this time in a more misogynistic culture? Doubt flooded over me. Rather than pushing the issue, I retreated.

"Of course," I replied, making one last halfhearted try. "But I've always wanted to run my own company, and this is a chance to operate a subsidiary and show you what I can do?" My closing argument was posed weakly as a question, making it easy for him to dismiss. With that, the matter was closed and he excused himself. Since I was inherently programmed to avoid dissension, we both knew that I would capitulate to his wishes.

I wanted to please my CEO and didn't like arguing with him—so I didn't pursue it. Wounded and deflated, I told myself that I was better off where I was. I was comfortable in my job, had very little risk, and could carry on enjoying my life.

> To my detriment, I used an overabundance of Feminine Energy caution

Today, I recognize how much Gender Pull was at work in this situation—both from my side as well as that of my CEO. We can only assume, but it is likely that he was impacted by Gender Pull and was operating from the unconscious bias that women shouldn't oversee the running of mines. Had I not been influenced by Gender Pull, I might have been more confident about my abilities and more ready to take the risk. I could have let people on the board know that I wanted the position, but instead, I chose to stay in the protective cocoon of my Feminine Energy and a role that I knew. I opted to use an overabundance of caution.

From Why to How

When you learn how to balance Masculine and Feminine Energies with Gender Physics, you will experience how it can propel you forward on the winding pathway to success. Getting there from where you are now will not happen overnight, but it is possible. In this chapter, we discussed why Gender Physics is important and why things are this way. In the next chapter, I give you lots of ideas for how to make gender physics a reality so that you can experience this yourself.

Use Gender Physics to Get Down to Business with This:

- Gender is a social construct.

- Living outside of gender expectations allows us to express ourselves freely as individuals.

- When people express their individuality, we can capitalize on their talent for greater business success.

- Gender Physics (using both gender energies) doubles the actions and options available to us, allowing us to choose the best action and option for every situation.

- Giving up either/or thinking that says we must be one or the other allows both our Masculine and Feminine Energies the freedom to emerge and work together.

- By seeing sameness, we can consider ourselves as human beings rather than as separate genders.

- Gender archetypes help us learn the ropes but should not be used as a prescription for how to live our lives.

- Gender Pull results from the unconscious bias that our behavior should reflect the stereotypical attributes of our biological gender.

- Those who are using both energies have the magnetic gift of presence—people are drawn to them and want to work with them.

- Balanced leaders are the best leaders.

- Using both your Masculine and Feminine Energies is like drawing water from the faucet: you add a little of each to find exactly the right temperature to suit your needs.

Chapter Two

Gender Physics: Becoming Whole

Feminine Energy Cares

Some people are naturals at using their energy to express themselves as individuals, and Bud, one of our customers when I worked for Potash Corporation of Saskatchewan (PotashCorp), was such a person. He was a big, tall, strapping guy—an oversized teddy bear with a soft demeanor and a humble manner. We jokingly called him our biggest customer, and he chuckled at this in his good-natured way. He ran a very successful operation, in no small part by collaborating, by always considering another's position, and by listening to find out what made everyone else tick—in short, he cared about others and built committed relationships.

When I first met Bud, he was with another customer and I was not sure who was who. I surreptitiously asked a colleague which customer came from which plant, and he said, "You'll always remember Bud because he is so likable and such a nice guy that you don't even notice what a smooth negotiator he is—he always walks away with the best pricing." How did he do it? Over time, I realized he was an expert at accessing his Feminine Energy. One day I got to experience that firsthand …

As a junior management person, I flew to St. Louis for an industry board meeting. After renting a car, I stopped by Bud's office en route for a quick visit. His plant was literally humming—a beehive of activity where people looked genuinely happy to be there. Many of the employees were even singing under their breath as they went about their duties. I swear there wasn't a frown in the place.

His Go-To Feminine Energy helped him build valuable connections

No one was in a hurry, everyone was smiling, and each passing person would pause at Bud's office to say hello and have a quick chat with whomever he had visiting. Bud was the epitome of an open-door manager. It was obvious that he cared about his employees, and they were unfailingly loyal to him.

"Can you stay tomorrow night in St. Louis?" he asked. "There's a ball game and I'd like you to come."

"Sure," I said. "Who's playing?" Bud stopped short of rolling his eyes, although he'd have been justified to do so, as it was one of the biggest games in baseball.

"It's the World Series and my team is playing." Laughing in his great big way, he turned to open the credenza, pulled out a red hat and coat, and said, "But you'll need to wear these to the game. You have to wear the team colors and show support for my beloved Cardinals!"

Receiving Bud's support and being his guest at the game was a real feather in my cap. To be included in such an event put me on an even keel with the large group of fertilizer people that Bud had put together. The fact that he accepted me gave me the credibility to earn others' respect as well.

Bud earned my undying devotion that day. His thoughtfulness and obvious pleasure in hosting the outing were typical of Feminine Energy. He genuinely enjoyed making other people happy. But he was not just a master relationship builder. He was also a brilliant tactician who analyzed his market and opened new plants in step with market demand, so he was able to access his Masculine Energy as well.

By strategically expanding through the years, Bud built his business into a small empire. He's a perfect example of a guy who uses Gender Physics and the best of both energies to not just meet but beat his goals.

Masculine Energy Confidently Steps Forward

If you naturally gravitate to Masculine Energy, you are probably pretty confident and not afraid to take a risk, especially when it is on behalf of those with less power. I was a lucky beneficiary of a CEO who did exactly that during a trip to Munich, Germany.

We sat in an aristocratic, elegant restaurant with heavy draperies, luxuriously upholstered chairs, and impeccable service. The CEO and I were there to meet with the senior executives of the German potash company that our company was in the process of acquiring. We all raised our glasses in a celebratory toast to the forthcoming union.

Earlier that afternoon, we had driven from one small German community to another, viewing operations that were taking place on the surface and meeting with each area's local plant managers. High on the hill overlooking each plant sat a grand mansion, a vestige of a different era. In a time when Germany was the only supplier of potash to the world, the mine manager would have lived in one of these homes and looked down on his little fiefdom. However, things change, and at the time of our visit, the German potash industry had long since been dwarfed by other world producers, which was why the German management team was now so keen to become a part of our company.

Over coffee at the end of the evening, we began to discuss plans for the upcoming day. The president of the German company turned to my CEO and advised him that they had an underground tour planned for him. Almost without pause, he turned to me with an ingratiating smile. "And my secretary has a delightful outing planned for you, too, Betty-Ann. She has arranged to take you on a tour of the city. Maybe you can do a little shopping together as well?"

Before I could check myself, my eyes widened a little, and immediately I felt heat rise to my cheeks—partly from anger and partly from the natural embarrassment of being excluded.

To his great credit, our CEO didn't skip a beat before stating firmly, "Sorry, your secretary will need to find someone else to accompany her shopping. Betty-Ann is a senior VP and officer of the company, and integral to this acquisition. It's important that she be along for a tour of the mine as well."

"But miners are a very superstitious bunch," the German potash president said, attempting to explain, "and I don't want to upset my men." He stammered on, "There is an old wives' tale that says that there will be a death if a woman goes underground." Then, shrugging his shoulders as though the matter were closed, he turned and smiled at me apologetically.

Slightly dumbfounded, I couldn't believe my ears. *Did he just imply that I'm a witch?* I thought to myself. I hesitated while gathering a suitable response, which gave my CEO a chance to demonstrate the honor and duty of Masculine Energy.

"That is unfortunate," he agreed. "Because I'm afraid if Betty-Ann is not welcome to go underground then I must decline your offer of a tour as well." And before an argument could arise, he confidently offered an alternative plan. "We really need to get back anyway, so why don't we come by the office in the morning for a coffee and debrief, and then we'll fly out afterward ... that way, Betty-Ann will be fully involved as well." With this answer, he avoided confrontation and stood up for his principles. He sent a definitive message that day that if he was involved, there would be equality for all his executives, regardless of gender.

He was someone who genuinely believed in fairness, but he was also defending his position. No one was going to imply that his executives were 'less than.' In this and other situations, I always admired how quickly he discerned when someone was undermining him personally and how adamantly he would guard his position. The adage "The best defense is a strong offense" would best describe his reactions and are typical of Masculine Energy.

When balanced, Masculine Energy protects others who may not have the same power base, using its courageous, confident nature to create a better world for all.

Balance Is Like Riding a Bicycle

Both Bud and my boss led with one energy or the other, yet each used balance to engender the loyalty of their staff and advance their agenda. As Albert Einstein said, "Life is like riding a bicycle. To keep your balance, you must keep moving."

On my sixth birthday, my dad and I walked down to the local department store in Strasbourg, Saskatchewan, where I picked out a brand-new two-wheeler bike. It was bright blue and I was excited. People in the city may have been using training wheels for years, but in the small town where I grew up, they hadn't yet arrived.

Dad and I wheeled the bike one block to the big backyard behind our hotel, and my mother came out to take our picture. That grainy black-and-white photo shows me proudly sticking out my chest holding the handlebars of my new two-wheeler. After it was taken, Dad told me to get on the bike and put my feet on the pedals. It was wobbly and scary, but I felt reassured because I knew that he was holding onto the bike to keep it steady.

Before I realized what was happening, he was running along behind me holding onto the seat, and hollering "Pedal hard, pedal hard!" Then with one last, big push I was on my own. I can still remember breathing hard and the feel of the bike as it swung first to the left and then to the right with me frantically pedaling to keep moving forward. It was a jerky ride and I was out of control—first leaning too far in one direction and then too far in the other. Eventually, I smashed into the back of the playhouse and hit the ground with a big thud.

Dad hurried to pick me up and dust me off. Then he put me back on the bike, and we did it again. After several failed attempts, suddenly everything just clicked. I was riding, and I was in total ecstasy. There I was, pedaling and adjusting, pedaling and adjusting, as my dad's words of encouragement grew fainter in the distance. I had done it. I had learned how to ride my bike. When I returned, my father hugged me, and I was on top of the world.

I talk about balance a lot in this book, and it is no different from learning to ride a bike. It takes a vision for what you want to accomplish, the courage to try, and the perseverance to get back on the bike and try again after each fall. Use the experience of riding a bike to advance your knowledge of the energies, visualize the balance between them, and experiment with using them yourself.

Different Energies in Different Situations

It shouldn't be a surprise that the male-dominated fertilizer company where I worked didn't suffer from a lack of Masculine Energy. This was to the organization's benefit when our mine managers competitively worked to outdo one another, each wanting to achieve the lowest production costs. Of course, if this energy wasn't balanced with caring for their employees they might have tried to reach these aims by compromising safety. That's why we started every management meeting by reviewing safety statistics to highlight their importance. And predictably, the mine managers made it a competition to see who had the best safety numbers as well!

Masculine Energy was also to our benefit if there was a crisis at one of our mines. We depended on someone to confidently step to the helm to set up a hierarchy, make critical decisions, and delegate the jobs to get the emergency under control as swiftly as possible. A crisis is not the time to call a group meeting to discuss the options and bring people to a consensus, as Feminine Energy wants to do.

But there are other times when Feminine Energy is really an advantage. For example, when you need to brainstorm a solution to a problem. This requires building upon one another's ideas and creating synergies. Feminine Energy is also important when you want to form a set of corporate values. Listening to others' opinions and bringing people to a consensus fosters a much greater buy-in. The last thing you want under these circumstances is a Masculine Energy person to call a meeting, sit down at the head of the table, and tell people what to believe.

Different Energies with Different Audiences

While working as a corporate executive, I came to realize that there was great value in using different energies depending on the audience I was addressing. For example, when communicating with people above my position, I would use considerably more Masculine Energy, which meant that I was direct, succinct, and looked unwaveringly at people as I spoke. This was most successful in situations such as defending my budget to the CFO or presenting a new program to the board. I found that when I spoke with confidence, they had confidence in me as well.

However, once I had the new program approved and went back to my department, it was important to inject more Feminine Energy into my communication style to encourage collaboration and teamwork. Instead of telling people how to do their jobs, I strove to tickle their creativity. By listening to their opinions and validating them, I was able to gather a wealth of ideas about possible ways of doing things. The added benefit is that when people feel accepted, trusted, and empowered, they will happily put in longer hours to make sure that things get done. They know that their supervisors and their team count on them and will not leave someone else holding the ball.

Different Energies Means Different Behaviors

If you look around your workplace, you will see examples of the two energies playing out, and you may even recognize some of these patterns in yourself. Consider what happens when you are part of a team that is celebrating the successful completion of an office project. Some people automatically step forward, cite their skills, and point out the important contributions they provided. Masculine Energy people are very comfortable promoting themselves. Conversely, acknowledging others is a Feminine Energy attribute. When the team reaches a milestone achievement, those who lead with Feminine Energy will often step back, never mentioning their individual contribution. Instead, they are quick to give the credit to everyone who worked on the project.

Of course, when taking advantage of new opportunities, things often don't go as planned. Those with Feminine Energy will react to failure by looking within and ruminating over what they could (or should) have done differently to change the outcome. Meanwhile, those with Masculine Energy will often react to failure by pointing to external factors and saying, "Business is business."

One time, I put out a news release to which the investment community reacted very negatively. Feeling totally responsible, I went to our CEO and told him that if I had presented the information differently it may not have had such an adverse reaction. He wouldn't allow me to accept responsibility. Instead, he laid the blame fully at the feet of the external audience. Clearly, I was approaching the situation from the Gender Pull of my Feminine Energy while he was totally in his Masculine Energy.

Balanced leaders, who are using Gender Physics, know their strengths and self-select projects where their attributes shine. When things go well, they accept praise for their contribution, yet always give credit to the team. However, when things don't go as hoped, they are quick to use their Feminine Energy to see what they could improve personally while also using their Masculine Energy to evaluate problems in the outside environment. Assessing both the internal and external limiting factors and learning from them enhances opportunities for future success.

Discovering Your Go-To Energy

While each of us is more successful when using a balance of both energies, one energy will likely feel more natural than the other. This is called our Go-To Energy, since when we approach situations we are most apt to turn to it first. Additionally, because it is the most familiar and the most comfortable, we are likely to consider it the most valuable and effective energy. It is no different from being right- or left-handed—one just feels better.

To discover your personal Go-To Energy, you can turn to the energy evaluation in Appendix 2. Alternatively, you can go through the list of attributes in Appendix 3 and choose the column of attributes that feels the most familiar to you. Remember that your Go-To Energy has nothing to do with your sexuality, although, as we have already learned, people often mistakenly equate the two.

Additionally, due to Gender Pull, approximately 70 percent of women and 70 percent of men will have a Go-To Energy consistent with their biological gender. Interestingly, age and occupation *do* influence the results. When conducting workshops, I found a higher propensity for Masculine Energy among women who are employed in the fields of engineering and law, where Masculine attributes are valued. Additionally, younger men (especially those who have taken paternity leave) are more apt to have a higher Feminine Energy score. This could be because our brains are plastic and, like chameleons, we adapt to our environment.

> Approximately 70 percent of us have a Go-To Energy consistent with our gender

It could also be the reason that my Go-To Energy is Masculine. I was probably inherently inclined that way, and then working in a male-dominated corporation reinforced it. A biologist I worked with would tease me by saying, "You know how women have the XX chromosome and men have the XY? Well, Betty-Ann, the bottom half has fallen off your last X because you're looking a lot like an XY."

Once you determine your Go-To Energy, recall a time when it served you well. As you recount the story, I am sure you will find that the success came because you inserted some of its opposite energy. Now think of a time when you used your Go-To Energy and things escalated out of control. You'll probably realize that there are consequences to not inserting the opposite energy and have the wisdom to know that there can be too much of a good thing.

Too Much Feminine Energy

While Feminine Energy can be a benefit when it causes us to reflect before taking action, that good thing can become a bad thing when used to excess.

I learned this as a young executive when I completed many special projects for a variety of senior managers. I didn't have to take on as much as I did, but I enjoyed the variety of challenges, was flattered that people would turn to me, and wanted to learn as much as I could. Besides, who knew where a project would lead?

It fit my belief that if you go for the responsibility first, then the title and money would follow. This strategy meant that I always had many things on my plate and was often on the run, packing as much into the day as possible.

One day, early in my career, I found myself sitting across from a young man of similar age and status. We had the same-sized office and did a lot of the same kind of work, except that he worked for the parent company and I was in sales.

At one point, I found myself in his office, drumming my fingers on his desk. Where was the RSVP list for the upcoming reception? Had he confirmed with the media and government which of their representatives would be attending? This contact was in his bailiwick, and I needed his input to keep the timing of my project on track.

> For those in extreme Feminine Energy, prioritizing activities hampers their ability to be emergent

But there he sat, reviewing vacation packages that I suspected he would never take. (The previous week, it was real estate. When I'd stopped by his office, he wanted to debate the pros and cons of various houses that

I doubted he would buy.) Inwardly, I rolled my eyes and held myself in check. I needed him to focus on the guest list and hound the invitees so that I could put together the table arrangements. It was high time to make things happen!

Then he said he was considering asking for a leave of absence. I was astounded. We were about to take the company public. He was responsible for key stakeholder relations, yet he was pondering taking time off? No wonder things in his department were in such disarray.

I shook my head and said, "You can't do this right now. It would be career suicide." However, I realized that he viewed his career the way he looked at houses or vacations. Every time he started to narrow the field and approach closure, he explored even more options.

His work style fit many other attributes of extreme Feminine Energy. When we worked on a program, it was impossible to get him to stick to the budget, as financial planning completely overwhelmed him. He didn't want to analyze anything and would rather just wait until something "felt right." Loath to prioritize activities, he didn't want to take away from his ability to be emergent. His lack of ability to follow through on practical details and important commitments meant that he came across as undisciplined, and it hurt his credibility.

He was charming and easy to talk to—people liked him since he always agreed with their position. But the closer you looked, the more it became apparent that he didn't have a position of his own. He didn't want to make a decision and didn't know what he stood for. He was not unlike Edith Bunker from the golden-oldie hit television show *All in the Family*. Edith agreed with everybody. She didn't have any opinions of her own. In fact, in one episode when asked if she believed in capital punishment, she answered, "Well, so long as it ain't too severe."

When you have too much Feminine Energy in an organization, people become immersed in their feelings, or paralyzed by the fear that taking action might offend someone. It is not uncommon to see them put their heads in the sand and do nothing, assuming it will all somehow work out. Too much Feminine Energy means deals don't get closed, decisions don't get made, and prospects aren't converted into clients.

It is also frustrating because those with too much Feminine Energy are indecisive. Such individuals will mull everything over for ages, considering every angle. Just when you think they are—at last—close to finalizing things, they call another meeting to discuss it further.

In corporate life, I frequently witnessed the impact of too much Feminine Energy, and due to Gender Pull, it was often displayed by women. When job responsibilities changed, many would wait, immobilized like a deer in the headlights, for someone else to instruct them on what to do next. When this happens, ultimately everyone suffers, production is hindered, and those who have not taken the initiative and seized the day lose the opportunity to be viewed as leaders.

Too Much Masculine Energy

Sometimes the competitive drive that Masculine Energy evokes can be taken too far. Picture the following with me.

A crisp morning. The sun was just peeking over an almost-black evergreen forest at the edge of a still lake. Only the sound of birds taking flight broke the almost ghostly silence as we arrived at the beach.

The shore was lined with a dozen brightly colored boats, and next to them, decked out in fishing gear, stood small groups of men. Each group consisted of one or two of our customers, a salesperson for our company, and their respective guides. Handshakes and good-natured salutations were exchanged as the contents of the boats were checked for, in order of importance, lures, beer, and lunch. It promised to be a good day to kick back and relax, discuss the markets, develop a little camaraderie, and hopefully reel in some big fish. You could almost hear a collective sigh of "Ah, life is good."

Looking out over our group, I smiled—it had been a productive few days. We had flown our customers into Saskatchewan that week, toured the mine, attended a few office presentations, and now we were finishing off the week with some fishing at one of our northern lakes. It was a great way to cement relationships with our key potash buyers.

As we waited to get started, the unmistakable sound of testosterone being dialed up interrupted the morning reverie. I cringed inwardly as our newly appointed head of sales began collecting money for a betting pool where the prize would go to whoever made the biggest catch of the day. Masculine Energy loves a hierarchy, and what better way to play one-upmanship than to create winners and losers?

> Overly focused on the short-term win, he was in too much Masculine Energy and created a long-term loss

The betting pool itself wasn't the problem—the problem was the guy who was organizing it. He hated to lose. Without fail, if he was charged with setting up a company golf tournament or bowling contest, his team would always be stacked with the best players. I knew that by the end of the day, somehow, the rules for the fishing derby would change to his advantage—which is exactly what happened.

When the boats pulled into the pier at five o'clock, the fish were weighed and—surprise! surprise!—guess who declared himself the winner? One of our largest buyers protested the slippery rules and took him to task. Our illustrious head of sales dismissed the protest and held his ground, much to the discomfort of us, his staff.

All the work, time, and effort that we had put into organizing the event and garnering goodwill went down the drain. The customer, a top buying executive for a large cooperative account, was ticked. Later, he advised my buddy Harry that if our company wanted to maintain his future business, he never wanted to see the head of sales in his office again.

So, an event that should have been a great relationship builder between our company and our customers was sullied by an overabundance of competitive Masculine Energy. Had our head of sales considered the customer's position, who wanted to win as much as he did, he might have developed some empathy and had a more balanced approach. Unfortunately, because he was unable to access some Feminine Energy and simply had to win, he lost a lot that day.

Ultimately, using both energies would have made him the winner. He might have lost the fishing derby, but he would have developed a loyal customer. Instead, he opted for the short-term satisfaction of a win and created a long-term loss. Don't get me wrong. There is nothing wrong with a little competition. It served our head of sales well in the marketplace, but he just didn't realize that this strength wasn't an advantage in every situation.

When Masculine Energy gets out of balance, people can become domineering and arrogant. They are prone to set up their own little kingdoms and establish themselves as monarchs. They belt out orders and have no tolerance for being questioned. With no long game, they have no impulse control, don't care who they hurt, and take action for the sake of action. Or they do things simply to try to set themselves apart—but it sometimes backfires. I recall a man who would stride purposefully around the office every day with his chest puffed out while looking at his watch as if he was on his way to an important meeting. He wasn't going anywhere in particular, but he wanted to differentiate himself and project an image of importance. The secretarial pool quickly caught on to his routine; instead of being viewed as important, he was ridiculed as silly.

Canadian businessman F. Ross Johnson, who took a run at RJR Nabisco in the late 1980s, is a perfect example of Masculine Energy run amok. He attempted one of the largest leveraged buyouts to that point in history. His story was told in a book, *Barbarians at the Gate*, and later was made into a movie. Johnson and his cohorts failed miserably, in part because someone sprinkled way too much Masculine Energy on their Wheaties.

Those with too much Masculine Energy can be addicted to action

Addicted to adrenaline and stirring things up, if there wasn't a deal in the works that day, the 'Barbarians' would manufacture action by reorganizing the office and changing the company's reporting structure. Employees would spend an entire day moving offices from one floor to another, studying the new organization chart, and reconfiguring their computers.

It created total chaos for their staff, who would go home utterly exhausted, but it was gratifying for those in charge, who had a desperate need for relentless, frenzied activity.

Keeping Strengths from Becoming Weaknesses

Each of the two energies has its strengths (or Virtues), and it is very easy to overuse these attributes. When looking back at our achievements, we will almost always give the credit to the characteristic(s) of our Go-To Energy that set us apart. We take pride in these attributes and wrap ourselves in them like a warm security blanket. It becomes natural to dial them up to the extreme when we are attached to the outcome and really want to demonstrate good performance.

However, when we go full out, all the time, it can get us into trouble. Take, for example, the office manager who values being a good relationship builder—assuredly a great attribute when used in moderation. Should they overdo it, however, and begin to accept lackadaisical work from direct reports in an effort to get along, they are bound to end up with lackluster results. Their strengths (or Virtues) become their weaknesses (or Vices).

Swinging to the Other Extreme

When people feel pushed out of their comfort zone, they are prone to not only dial up their Go-To Energy to the extreme but also swing to the extreme of their opposite energy. It's like the ride commonly seen in amusement parks, the one in the shape of a ship. It swings high into the air in one direction, and once it reaches its apex, everyone holds their breath because they know what is coming: a drop and fast ride in the other direction.

This level of unbalance in our lives can come when we feel diminished, dismissed, or denied. Typically, we hold our breath and frantically search for something a regain our balance—we don't want to stay suspended in a state of discomfort, just hanging in the air—so we push back. Unfortunately, this push can bring us to the opposite extreme.

We see this in Walter White, the main character in the hit television show *Breaking Bad*. In the opening season, White is a mild-mannered and submissive chemistry teacher. Everything about him is placating and defeated: his eyes, his voice, and even his posture. The first few episodes reveal that his passiveness isn't new—he was once a promising chemist who caved in to a business partner and lost a fortune. He was further humiliated when his wife ran off with the guy who milked him. Plodding along as a teacher, he receives a diagnosis of terminal lung cancer and realizes that his family will be left with nothing when he dies. He feels shame, as though he has given his whole life and has become a doormat, a victim of society for his trouble.

These are the circumstances that transform him into a dominant aggressor. The pendulum of his life swings from one extreme to the other, where he finds himself thwarting anyone who interferes with his drug dealing. It is impossible to turn away from the mesmerizing formation of a ruthless monster as White grows his roving meth lab into a monopoly and becomes a kingpin in the drug trade. Even the name of the series does not bode well for him—to "break bad" is to defy authority and/or the law, especially for personal gain. By rejecting social and moral norms, he follows this path, regardless of the ethics, and uses it to shift from perceived inferiority to fabricated superiority.

White's character began as a loving husband, father, and teacher, but he lived in an extreme Feminine Energy state to the point of being used and abused by others. Had he inserted some Masculine Energy and stood up for himself, first with his business partner and later within the school system, he could have found balance and avoided swinging from one extreme to the other.

Consider the Complement

Virtues can become Vices through overuse, but the great news is that they can be turned back into Virtues. Simply insert an appropriate attribute from the Complementary Energy, which is opposite. Most of us are reluctant to adopt our opposite traits because we have been conditioned to place a high value on our personal strengths and to consider them the superior and only option.

For example, if we pride ourselves on being upfront and direct, we may find it difficult to see the value in our being reserved and reticent. But it is the use of such combinations that will make us more successful. Similarly, those prone to action will fare better when they stop for reflection, as will those who insert a little caution into their confidence.

Consider the contrasting attributes of Feminine and Masculine Energies as differing colors. Philosopher Aristotle discovered that when one color was placed beside another, proximity changed the appearance of each. Later, artist Leonardo da Vinci observed that the finest harmonies occurred between colors that were exactly opposed. Eventually, with the development of the color wheel, the term "complementary color" was coined.

Just as this interplay between colors truly makes each color stand out, so it is with us. When we use the attributes from the two seemingly opposing Masculine and Feminine Energies and move dynamically between them, we can truly shine. That's the value of the Complement.

Below, you will find the Complementary Energy wheel, which provides a high-level view of the two energies. Feminine Energy attributes are in black and directly across are the complements of each, which are the Masculine Energy attributes in gray. Together they offer the best energy combination.

Complementary Energy Wheel

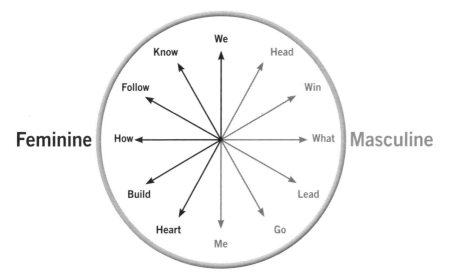

Here is an example using *Build* and its opposite, *Win*: Those with too much Feminine Energy tend to overapologize. They do this in an effort to build goodwill, since apologies reorganize the power hierarchy and make others feel more comfortable. But saying sorry can become a bad habit. When people apologize unnecessarily, they can put themselves permanently in a 'power-under' position. By introducing the complement (opposite on the energy wheel), they'll recognize their losing position and consider the importance of raising their status through winning. Wanting a win will motivate them to keep their apologies in check and will balance their behavior. They don't give up apologizing altogether; they just enhance their presence by doing it with more discretion.

On the opposite side of the energy wheel are those who have too much Masculine Energy. They always want to win, so they do not readily apologize or admit fault. An apology makes us indebted, at least for a short while, to another person, which these people avoid because they want power over others. They view an apology as a loss and they want to win. When those with too much Masculine Energy are forced to apologize, they will often place the other person in the wrong: "I'm sorry if YOU were offended." By introducing their Complementary Energy of *Build*, they'll recognize the importance of establishing better relationships. This will make them more open to examining their own behavior and give them the wisdom to apologize more routinely.

I cannot stress enough that you should be seeking to use your complement more often. While it is easiest and most expedient to go directly across the wheel and use the exact opposite attribute, sometimes you may choose a Virtue from another category (or Variable) since they can be mixed and matched. Imagine a manager who is resigned to the fact that they must fire someone but does it with respect and sensitivity, or the business owner who readily accepts responsibility for a mistake and rectifies the problem with their customer in an empathetic manner. People who use their Complementary Energy to balance their Go-To Energy become better at what they do and are also perceived as better. This applies to all the Variables and their subset of Virtues, but using it takes experimentation and practice—just like learning to balance and ride a bike.

Experiment with the Energies

I am no stranger to experimentation, as I have always loved to do things by trial and error. As a child, I mixed together household cleaners to see how they would react and poured peroxide over pennies just to watch the copper change color.

It is probably quite natural that, later, I would consider the various ways to advance my career as an experiment as well. But my approach didn't involve teams of scientists, systematic investigations, or reams of data. Instead, my experimental forays were personal and informal, more like sampling a variety of wines to find a favorite.

I would try things on, and if they didn't work, I would evaluate the outcome, adjust my approach, and carry on. This included weighing the results of face-to-face conversations, analyzing the interactions between individuals, and observing the ongoing narrative of organizations where I worked. It also included questioning the rules that society lives by and discovering the processes that bind or separate groups.

Early on, I recognized that not every experiment would be a success and that I had to put the negative experiences behind me and forge ahead. Rather than consider them failures, I simply treated them as useful data for future consideration. In that context, they became lessons and opportunities for growth.

Approaching my career as an experiment made me far more willing to venture into untested waters and try new things. This approach led me to experiment with the energies and ultimately to develop my Gender Physics theory.

I invite you to explore and discover. Experimenting with the energies will allow you to step outside your comfort zone and discover another part of yourself. Get on the bike and ride—experiment with a wider range of being.

Variables, Virtues, and Vices

The following chapters help you learn not only how to identify your strengths but also how to recognize when they have morphed into weaknesses. They include examples of utilizing different energy combinations and discuss the tools you can pull from the Gender Physics tool bag. Experimenting with these tools will keep your Virtues from becoming Vices and will help you unlock the energy you never knew you had to get the results you want.

Here are the basics: There are six Variable categories, each expressing an overarching Feminine or Masculine Energy principle, such as the desire to be either part of a group or an individual (*We/Me*), or the desire to make decisions based on emotions or on logic (*Heart/Head*). Each Variable has five sub-categories that are of a similar nature, which are the Feminine or Masculine Virtues. These are consistently presented with Feminine Energy on the left and Masculine Energy on the right.

You may notice that you lean toward Masculine Energy in one Variable category yet favor Feminine Energy in another, which is not surprising because we are all individuals made up of a medley of features. For instance, although your Go-To Energy may be Masculine and you are very action oriented (Masculine Energy) in the *Know/Go* Variable, you may discover that you clearly love the creative process (Feminine Energy) in the *How/ What* Variable.

Additionally, these attributes do not occur in isolation and are not absolutes. For example, I was once in a meeting where I felt heard and validated when our management team was making an important decision, so I felt *included*. However, after the meeting our management team went golfing, and due to antiquated rules women couldn't tee off until after 2 p.m., so my group was held back until the clock showed the magic time. This made me feel *excluded*, but did not negate the other. Seemingly polar opposites can exist together.

While I have provided a word to describe each Virtue (and, when overdone, Vice), please remember that these definitions aren't fixed. For example, *enable* is used here as a Vice, defined as someone who supports another in unhealthy practices. Yet an enabler can also be someone who encourages staff to express their ideas or enables another to get an education. Thus, I would ask that you not get hung up on the limitations of language but rather accept the spirit and sentiment of the words as intended and described.

Note also that some of these words could fit in a few different Variables. For example, in the Feminine Energy Vice someone could be *confused* when working in a flat organization structure because without clear leadership it is hard to know what to prioritize (*Build/Win*). However, they could also be *confused* as to whether to follow their *intuition* in the *Heart/Head* Variable.

And finally, this process is about helping you to become more aware of how it feels to get out of balance—the word choices are not set in stone. You may prefer other words to describe the Vices, and that is just fine. If a word doesn't feel right, I invite you to find a new one by filling in the blanks in this statement: *When I am too much in the Virtue of* _____, *I am in danger of becoming* _____.

To summarize:

- The core elements of Gender Physics are Feminine Energy and Masculine Energy.
- These two energies can be expressed by six different Variables.
- Each Variable has five Virtues that become Vices when dialed up to the extreme.

Get on the Bike and Ride

In Gender Physics, as in riding a bike, balance is important, but it's not static. It requires nuanced movements left or right to maintain an upright position while moving forward. In Gender Physics our leaning toward left or right is leaning toward Feminine or Masculine Energy. We pedal first with Feminine Energy and then with Masculine. With time, we will gain confidence about when to pedal, when to glide, and when to adjust. Eventually, we will shift between energies so smoothly that we won't even think about it. As we are naturally using both energies, we'll simply conclude, "This is just me being me." And ... it is!

Use Gender Physics to Get Down to Business with This:

- Feminine Energy is other-oriented, values all opinions, cares, and sets up flat organizations.

- Masculine Energy confidently steps forward, is motivated by competition, and favors hierarchical structure.

- Masculine Energy is most effective when used 'up the chain' with those above you and Feminine Energy when used 'down the chain' with direct reports.

- Each of us has a natural Go-To Energy that we turn to first.

- Your Complementary Energy is your Go-To Energy's seemingly opposite energy, and using it makes the latter shine brighter.

- To accomplish your goals, lead with the best energy for every situation, audience, and venue, and insert its Complementary Energy for balance.

- When Masculine or Feminine Energy is used to the proper degree, it is a strength, or Virtue.

- When a Virtue is overused, it becomes a weakness, or Vice.

- A Vice can be turned back into a Virtue by inserting a Complementary Energy attribute.

- We can experiment to find balance—the same way we learned to ride a bike.

Chapter Three

We/Me Variable

Alone we can do so little; together we can do so much.

—*Helen Keller*

Characteristics of the Feminine Energy *We* and the Masculine Energy *Me*

- In the *We* Variable, Feminine Energy wants to be part of a group.
- In the *Me* Variable, Masculine Energy seeks to be set apart.

- In the *We* Vices, those with Feminine Energy acquiesce to the group and lose their personal identity.
- In the *Me* Vices, those with Masculine Energy suffer from human detachment.

- When practicing Gender Physics and using both energies, people maintain what makes them unique while forming alliances.

Typical Features of the Two Energies in This Variable

Feminine Energy: *We*	Masculine Energy: *Me*
Sees the power of the group and constantly searches for cohesiveness	Sees the value of being unique and looks to be set apart
Believes that the whole is greater than the sum of its parts	Recognizes individual contribution and protects territory
Enjoys being a member of a group (a troupe of dancers or choir of singers)	Likes to be center stage (solo performer)
Wants to include everyone and believes there is strength in numbers	Believes that the best chance of survival depends on acting independently
Finds the courage to do things for others but is less courageous on own behalf	Wants to put individual mark on things
Sacrifices personal preference for what is best for the group as a whole	Serves self first and wants freedom of choice
Is energized by images of harmony with others and consults with others before making a decision	Is proud of self-sufficiency and trusts own instincts
Indicates relation to others in personal introductions (I am in investor relations at PotashCorp.)	Cites individual accomplishments in personal introductions (I am a senior VP at PotashCorp.)

We Is the Wagon Train and *Me* Is the Lone Ranger

In this Variable, those with Feminine Energy enjoy working as part of an *integrated* group where everyone is equal. Watching spaghetti westerns in my youth, I always admired the *collective* of the wagon train (*We*). Their members aligned with one another to make such decisions as how far to travel each day, who would keep watch, and who would cook meals. Working seamlessly together, they accepted the stated protocol of gathering up bedrolls at dawn, traveling at a speed that suited everyone, and settling in for the night by circling the wagons. Every action considered *others* and was made by *consensus* in recognition that there was safety in numbers. They understood that crossing the open and often dangerous prairie to arrive at their destination necessitated taking care of one another. Individuals give up their independence to make their *inclusive* environment successful.

I was also awed by the *autonomous* and self-sufficient Lone Ranger, sitting high in the saddle at the top of the hill and epitomizing the Virtues of Masculine Energy (*Me*). It was important to him to *differentiate* himself from the group and be acknowledged for his *individual* attributes. He liked the freedom of acting in his own *self-interest*, deciding independently where he was going and how long he would take to get there. Lone Rangers don't want the responsibility of the group, preferring to ride solo and depend *exclusively* on their own wits and self-determination. This allows them to operate separately, doing their own scouting. And they aren't afraid to have a shoot-out to test their skill against another individual gunslinger.

We and *Me* Working Together with Gender Physics

The attributes of the Lone Ranger didn't die with the spaghetti westerns. They are alive and well in our business world, where many CEOs seek to be seen as charismatic individuals with the focus on them rather than on their companies. Consider General Electric's former CEO Jack Welch, who promoted himself by sharing his personal philosophies on such topics as university tenure, the country's tax rates, work-life balance, people's wealth expectations, and even chewing gum! Given our reality-TV world and the powerful position business holds in our economy, it's not surprising that for many CEOs their egos get the best of them and they fall into the Vice of narcissism. Unfortunately, too often the brand the CEO develops isn't beneficial for the company and comes at its expense.

In Gender Physics, CEOs can be seen as strong individuals, yet they use their celebrity status to advance the collective. Steve Jobs demonstrated this when he came back to a failing Apple Inc. eleven years after having been fired. The company had only 4 percent market share, had incurred losses of over $1 billion a year, and was just a few months away from insolvency. It would have been easy for him to turn and walk away; instead, he gathered the Apple employees together and told them that while the company made boxes very well, that wasn't who they were at their core—they were all about people with passion coming together to change the world for the better. With those words, Jobs inspired the disheartened Apple employees, and they collectively rose to the occasion: within a few short years, working in concert, they made Apple the world's most valuable publicly traded company. Jobs epitomized the best of the Lone Ranger, who stepped up to the occasion to lead and direct the wagon train at a critical time, thereby demonstrating the true balance of Gender Physics.

Too much ego can result in the Masculine Energy Vice of narcissism

Getting to Know the Virtues, and Their Vices

In the *We/Me* Variable, the overarching desire of Feminine Energy people is to 'find a tribe,' while those who prefer Masculine Energy want individual freedom. Each can be expressed by five related Virtues, which are strengths when used in appropriate amounts but, when used in absolute terms, can morph into Vices, or weaknesses.

We Virtues (Feminine Energy Strengths)	*Me* Virtues (Masculine Energy Strengths)
Collective	Individual
Integration	Differentiation
Inclusive	Exclusive
Other-oriented	Self-interest
Consensus	Autonomy

We Virtues (Feminine Energy Strengths)	*We* Vices (Feminine Energy Weaknesses)
Collective	Cult
Integration	Herding
Inclusive	Homogenization
Other-oriented	Loss of self
Consensus	Dependency

Me Virtues (Masculine Energy Strengths)	*Me* Vices (Masculine Energy Weaknesses)
Individual	Narcissism
Differentiation	Segregation
Exclusive	Prejudice
Self-interest	Egocentric
Autonomy	Disconnected

Analyzing YOU

In Appendix 2, the Go-To Energy Evaluation, total your scores separately in each part for questions 1 to 5 (inclusive). If your score is higher in part 1, you operate from Feminine Energy *We* in this Variable. If your score is higher in part 2, your behavior is Masculine Energy *Me* in this Variable.

Collective/Individual Virtues

Do you like meat and potatoes served separately or mixed together as stew?

Virtue Feminine	Vice Feminine	Virtue Masculine	Vice Masculine
Collective	Cult	Individual	Narcissism

I remember one board meeting that went well past the time estimated on the agenda, and naturally, we executives waiting at the reception were very curious as to what was being discussed. Eventually, Brett, a friend and colleague who had been in the meeting, came with an update. "You wouldn't believe what Bob has done now." Bob, our CEO, was good at getting what he wanted. He often played a high-stakes game—acting first and asking for forgiveness later. With his confident and smooth demeanor, he had managed to get away with this throughout his career. Nothing Bob did would surprise me, and I waited for Brett to elaborate.

"First, he purchased an expensive membership for himself at a men's only golf club. Then, without board approval, he arranged for the head of the compensation committee to sign off on it as a company expense."

We all knew that he had strategically placed his long-time friend, confidant, and godfather to his son on the board to assist him. In turn, the board had made Bob's pal chair of the compensation committee, which gave him some leeway in signing off on such expenses, even if it were a gray area. However, this didn't pass the 'smell test.' "The board is not happy," Brett said, "and although they made their feelings known, eventually they gave in and approved it."

As a woman in management, the entire situation irritated me. I could not fathom a good business reason for our company to be paying for a golf membership at a course where women couldn't play. This meant that not only women from our company were excluded but also our women suppliers and investors. It sent a very bad signal. This injustice made me very angry; it was just one more situation where women would not be dealt a fair hand as we sought our place at the table. Our CEO already had a golf membership at a well-established and prestigious coed club that met the company's needs, and I strongly felt that our company should eliminate all systemic prejudice, including men-only clubs.

At the reception later, I overheard grumbling chatter from those who had been present at the board discussion. Someone pointed out that even women on the board wouldn't be allowed to play at the club. Someone else said that the company had a publicly stated diversity policy and that this decision contradicted those directives.

This story demonstrates the type of conflict that can arise between people coming from a *collective* mindset and those who operate from an *individual* mindset. Our CEO, out of balance in his Masculine Energy, had focused solely on himself. He did not appear to consider or care about the ramifications of his decisions on others or the policies that were established to serve the organization as a whole.

Although there were a few emerging women leaders, at the time, I was the only senior woman executive. We were all keenly aware, however, that our male colleagues were invited to golf while we were often excluded. Not long after the board meeting, Bob invited some investors and analysts to golf at his men-only course, which meant that I was not included even though they were my clients. This was not only dismaying but also discouraging: it left me feeling far less enthusiastic and committed to the company. While it wasn't enough for me to quit and walk out the door, it became another straw that would eventually break the camel's back.

The Feminine Energy Vice creates 'group think' in the boardroom

Too much in his Masculine Energy, Bob was overly *individualistic*. If you focus too much on yourself, you can develop tunnel vision, creating the Masculine Energy Vice of *narcissism*. In this Vice, he became totally self-absorbed in his own wants and needs. In turn, he eroded the confidence of many board members and lost the trust of many women in the organization. The pendulum had swung too far one way.

In swinging too far the other way, there is danger of giving up too much of yourself, and you enter the Feminine Energy Vice of *cult* behavior. In this mob mentality, you'll make too many sacrifices for the group and find your identity with them, rather than as an individual. When too much value is placed on those who speak our same language and express similar views, it encourages what is commonly called 'group think' in the boardroom.

If our CEO had infused his *individualism* with some concern for the *collective*, he would have been far more effective in his role. Ideally, when you become more cognizant of and adept at accessing Gender Physics, you'll use both Masculine and Feminine Energy to take care of yourself, but always with consideration for the organization.

Integration/Differentiation Virtues

Ever seen someone whose toenails are all painted red except the little one, which is painted gold?

Virtue Feminine	Vice Feminine	Virtue Masculine	Vice Masculine
Integration	Herding	Differentiation	Segregation

In the 1970s, Western society was concerned about the population explosion and one magazine cover after another asked, "Will there be enough food for the world to eat?" Growing more food for a growing world population demanded fertilizer, and people in the industry viewed themselves as heroes—a position they thoroughly enjoyed. Thirty years later, the public had forgotten about the population explosion and became concerned about the environment. There was a heightened focus on the risks of both producing and applying fertilizer, and our industry moved from being the good guys in white hats to the bad guys in black hats.

Faced with a major public perception problem, an industry committee was convened to review the issue, which I attended on behalf of our company. I listened to earnest entreaties of supportive researchers as they discussed the many benefits of fertilizer that were being buried in the negative media rhetoric. I appreciated their passion but knew their long dissertations would be lost in the world of thirty-second sound bites.

We needed a wide-reaching advertising campaign that would remind the public of our product's benefits. While it was discussed and considered, there was little appetite amongst the cash-strapped fertilizer companies to take on something of this nature. The various company representatives shook their heads, sighed deeply, and went back to their regular jobs.

I admit that the problem was a bit overwhelming, but my interest had been spurred. Back at the office, I met with our advertising agency, and we planned a grassroots campaign with simple and digestible messages that could be delivered by our network of dealers. Then we planned a meeting where the dealers would hear a panel of experts present their best sound bites. It was a risk, but we counted on our ability to draw the sound bites from the experts and the openness of the dealers not only to accept what they heard but also to willingly deliver the messages. In my best moments, I assured myself that our cost-effective scheme was brilliant; in my worst, I feared I'd be orchestrating a humiliating flop.

The panel didn't start out a barn burner, but then one of the experts said, "If you have lots of food, you have lots of problems, but if you have no food, you have only one problem." It was like a bolt of electricity shot through the room. Everyone suddenly sat up in their chairs, nodding their heads in agreement. That was only one of the many effective sound bites heard at the table that day, and the dealers left ready to convincingly spread our message to the world. The "Fertile Minds" program was born.

Use Masculine Energy to differentiate yourself from the competition

Back home, the guys I worked with were thrilled. They were like little kids at a birthday party hopping up and down and rubbing their hands with glee. In one bold move, we had successfully *differentiated* ourselves from the competition and positioned ourselves as a leader.

We ran this highly successful program for another four rewarding years, and our competitors eyed it jealously each time we ran a fresh event. It was probably inevitable that the industry would want to take it over. When a new leader joined their association, he was determined that the program be *integrated* within the industry rather than belonging to just one company. When he came to talk to me about it ("I know this is your baby … I don't blame you for wanting to hang on to it …"), I am sure that he expected me to dig in and resist.

However, the meeting didn't take long—I agreed quickly. He was probably surprised at how easily I gave it up and offered my full endorsement. A big part of me hated to see it go, since running such a high-profile program was a heady experience. I wondered at the time if I had hit my career peak and whether it would all be downhill thereafter. But I knew that letting go was the right decision.

Consistent with the principles of Gender Physics, we developed this program by *differentiating* ourselves, but ultimately, the most value came when we *integrated* with our competitors. Had we resorted to extreme Feminine Energy, we could have bought into the widely held belief that nothing could be done about the situation, and along with the rest of the world, could have allowed ourselves to be *herded* by the negative public opinion.

Use Feminine Energy to integrate with others to achieve a collective advantage

We also didn't take *differentiation* to the Masculine Energy extreme whereby we *segregated* the program and kept it for ourselves. With the entire industry behind it, the program was more successful and influenced more people—and in tandem with others, our company still benefited. We believed in the proverb, "A rising tide lifts all boats." What was good for our industry was good for us.

A final addendum that proves the value of using Gender Physics to balance the energies: when I retired, the industry association leader approached me and said, "Betty-Ann, in our business I've watched lots of people come and go, but you are leaving a valuable legacy."

Inclusive/Exclusive Virtues

Remember the iconic scene of the animated character Daffy Duck when he grabbed onto a large pearl and with crazy eyes said, "Mine, mine, mine ..."?

Virtue Feminine	Vice Feminine	Virtue Masculine	Vice Masculine
Inclusive	Homogenization	Exclusive	Prejudice

At the age of twenty-one, I accepted a position with a major brewing company as their first female sales representative—not just for our province but for the entire country. Not surprisingly, my male colleagues were less than thrilled with the prospect of a woman appearing on their turf—and a young one at that. At my first major assignment, a gopher derby in the small town of Eston, Saskatchewan, these men made their opinions bitingly clear. They were an *exclusive* group and had no intention of making it *inclusive* with me.

We were supposed to travel to the derby together from Saskatoon on the morning of the event. I anxiously awaited the sound of tires on the driveway that would signal the arrival of my coworkers to pick me up.

The pickup time, 9 A.M., came and went. So did 9:10, then 9:20, and finally 9:30. As each minute painfully passed, my heart sank further. Desperately wanting to be *included*, I slowly came to the realization that I had been *excluded*. The men had left me behind.

I was humiliated and felt the heat of deep shame crawl over my scalp and down my neck. On a rational level, I knew I had no reason to be embarrassed. But my gender socialization and the voice in my head joined together and the questions started:

Why did I feel I deserved to be there at all? Who was I to challenge the status quo? What made me think that I had what it took or deserved to be part of the group? It took all that I had not to go back to bed and curl up in a fetal position.

At 9:45, I knew without a doubt that I had been deliberately abandoned, and that was the moment I made a life-shifting decision. I stepped into my Masculine Energy and climbed into my car, determined to make it to the event on my own. As it turned out, I didn't have to hurry because I handily beat my colleagues, who had stopped along the way for refreshments. Upon arrival, I quickly set to work, good-naturedly taking on any task that the harried local organizers threw my way. I flipped burgers and readied the little gophers for their races. The participants were happy for my help; I was happy to open my brand of beer for them.

Masculine Energy gave me the courage to take a risk

When my fellow representatives eventually did show up, they were surprised to find me well established with the event organizers, busily promoting our product with all my new friends. When they saw their clients accept me, they happily claimed me as one of their own.

This experience was an early exercise in using both energies. I had to muster up Masculine Energy to take the risk to get in the car and drive to the derby on my own. Taking that action was completely outside my comfort zone, but I inherently understood that it was a critical step in proving my mettle.

Then I had to remind myself that the reason I had been hired was that I had good people skills. That made me *exclusively* qualified for the job. Once I arrived in Eston, I put those skills to work learning people's names, hearing their stories, and sharing jokes with them. My Feminine Energy service-orientation meant that I was *included* as one of the group.

Looking back, I realize that when I had first started with the company, I simply wanted to blend in and become a *homogeneous* member of the group. It felt safer to be in that Feminine Energy Vice. However, had I arrived with my colleagues and just hung with them, my light would have been hidden under a bushel and my value would not have been recognized. As fate would have it, being left behind forced me to develop my Masculine Energy quickly, and that, in turn, highlighted my skills and attributes.

The Masculine Energy Vice of *exclusiveness* is *prejudice*, where you discriminate against others and deliberately enforce separation and isolation. Interestingly, we often see this behavior displayed by those who themselves feel threatened and are using it to defend their position or territory, as in the actions of my colleagues toward me.

> Blending in and becoming homogeneous will hide your light under a bushel

Thanks to Gender Physics, I used a combination of both energies, which not only furthered my career experiment but also worked to my advantage.

Other-Oriented/Self-Interest Virtues

Know that guy who laughs at all his own jokes without caring if others like them?

Virtue Feminine	Vice Feminine	Virtue Masculine	Vice Masculine
Other-oriented	Loss of self	Self-interest	Egocentric

My first year at PotashCorp, I was handed responsibility for our company's corporate presence at the annual dealers' convention. This came with a preexisting tradeshow booth, highly Masculine in style: large, company-focused, and haloed by a giant *P* that rotated in a circle above the chest-thumping copy below. Plenty of money had been invested into the building, shipping, and storing of the booth, which I dutifully sent off to the convention center in Las Vegas.

Once there, standing in the booth next to the table of untouched company brochures, I immediately recognized the error and spent the bulk of the show staring forlornly around the empty convention hall. You could have shot a cannon down those aisles and not hit a single soul. I felt like someone who had arrived for a party on the wrong day. Except I did, sort of, have company. The booths of other companies to my right and left were inhabited by equally uncomfortable and lonely representatives.

It wasn't hard to discern the whereabouts of the missing crowd: I could hear their jovial laughter in the distance. After a quick trip around the tradeshow floor, the attendees slipped away and were now congregated in the lobby coffee shop. Keen to interact with the customers, our salesmen had quickly followed.

Fidgeting from one foot to the other, I had a lot of time to survey our expensive booth and marvel at the money wasted. I vowed to abandon the booth—and all its accompanying expenses—for next year's convention.

When the tradeshow rolled around again—this time in New Orleans—I informed my sales team that we were leaving our booth behind. My colleagues were incredulous. Abandoning our booth, they argued, would squash our ability to fly our flag. Their strong resistance did make me question my decision. It was tempting to simply follow accepted protocol and ship the booth. We'd be aligned with every other company there, and there was little risk in doing what the guys wanted. I understood their position, but unlike them, I didn't think it was in our *self-interest*. Deep down, I felt there was a better way to do it.

Mustering some Masculine Energy courage, I said, "Who cares about the booth—our customers don't. They want to drink coffee and socialize, so I'm bringing the coffee to them." Making this decision was based on my use of *other-oriented* Feminine Energy. I considered not what would make us feel good but, rather, what our customers wanted. Then I used my Masculine Energy to set in motion the activities to get it done.

Balancing our Masculine Energy *self-interest* and Feminine Energy *other-orientation*, we created a superior outcome

Knowing that New Orleans is famous for its beignets (a lovely doughnut that pairs particularly well with coffee), I hunted down a catering company with great reviews, hired them, and then rented chairs and tables for our booth. Upon arrival in New Orleans, I erected a sign heralding the free coffee and beignets available at the PotashCorp booth, laid out our company brochures, and then stood back and waited.

Soon enough, our booth was full to bursting with bodies. Chatting men, eager to give their feet a rest from the concrete floors of the convention center, content with a beignet in one hand and a coffee in the other, relaxed in their chairs. The booth teemed with energy and rocked with laughter, and our salespeople effortlessly worked the room. Of course, we still had some *P* logo signage and made sure that no one left without a company brochure. Our interaction at the conference could not have been better, and those colleagues who had previously questioned (and criticized) my plan were more than delighted.

It was the use of the Feminine Energy *other-orientation* that spurred this victory, but had I allowed this Virtue to be dialed up to the extreme, the objective of making our customers happy could have gotten entirely out of balance. We would not have shown our logo or been so diligent about still talking business and being sure that everyone left with a company brochure. Instead of focusing on our objective, which was to promote our company in a way that was amenable to our customers, it would have resulted in the Vice of *loss of self*.

Our salespeople who only cared about the big rotating *P* were in danger of falling into the Masculine Energy Vice of too much *self-interest*, which results in being *egocentric*. Thinking of only what you want or what makes you feel better is not the way to ingratiate yourself as a customer's supplier. It is important to balance your *self-interest* with *other-orientation* before it spirals out of control and becomes counterproductive.

This tradeshow experience made a name for us at the convention, and I credit that to the use of Gender Physics. It was in our company's *self-interest* to stand out at the convention, but it would not have happened without focusing first on the *other* to discern what our customers really wanted.

Consensus/Autonomy Virtues

Do you order pepperoni pizza when everyone else agrees to order a Hawaiian pizza?

Virtue Feminine	Vice Feminine	Virtue Masculine	Vice Masculine
Consensus	Dependency	Autonomy	Disconnected

Early in my career, one of my volunteer projects was helping to choose the Educator of the Year in my home city. People from all over the city nominated individuals whom they felt had been an important teacher in their lives. It could be someone in the school system, but nominees also included babysitters, First Nations Elders, sports coaches, and choir directors. Typically, I would receive the package of nominations on a Friday and spend the weekend reading it through. On the following Monday afternoon, the committee would come together to choose the year's winners.

I often referred to it as a 'three boxes of Kleenex weekend' because so many of the nominators told such heartwarming stories of the unsung heroes living in our community. I would cry (and often sob) as I read the stories of people who acted generously, and without expectation of return or reward—to make a difference in the lives of others. By doing so they accomplished much, including brightening the world for children with disabilities and rescuing women from prostitution. Every testimonial was touching and inspiring, and in most cases, the award presented an isolated opportunity to recognize their good deeds. As you can imagine, every nomination was more than worthy, and in spite of there being many categories, narrowing it down to a winner in each was a daunting endeavor. The responsibility of choosing weighed heavily on our committee.

For the woman who headed the committee, the easiest thing to do would have been to convene the meeting, take a vote, and send us on our way. That approach would have allowed us to each express our *autonomous* opinion through a vote, but it may not have garnered the best result. Instead, we sat around the table and had a detailed discussion about every nomination. As we talked about the significance of each candidate's contribution, we often found ourselves looking at the nominees in a new light. Some we might have previously overlooked rose to the surface.

Ultimately, after much talk, it would become clear which candidate was the best choice, and we reached a *consensus* on who should win in each category. The wide cross section of people at the table could have made reaching a consensus difficult, but because everyone participated and every opinion was treated equally, we would leave these meetings feeling very settled in our collective decisions. It would never have worked if there wasn't full respect for all the opinions or if one was viewed as more important than the others. But that was never the case since we were exercising our Feminine Energy.

> Using Feminine Energy, everyone was treated equally and we readily reached a consensus

In this instance, reaching a *consensus* with Feminine Energy worked because we were willing to take the time to really process. Yet there are times when a more *autonomous* Masculine

Energy approach is needed. For example, when the *Titanic* is sinking, that is not the time to gather everybody at the table for a long discussion to decide on a course of action. When speed is of the essence, someone needs to lead the group and autonomously make the decision.

Those who lean too far into their Feminine Energy can become *dependent* on others for a decision. In this Vice, they want so badly to be part of the group that they lose their individual autonomy and often give up their integrity to help the group reach a consensus. While developing relationships is intrinsic to our very nature, if we make them the most important item on our agenda, we give away too much of ourselves.

Masculine Energy leaders who ignore others in the decision-making process, especially when there is ample time for consultation, are likely to become emotionally *disconnected* from their team. When in this Vice, the leader limits participation, and the valuable and diverse input of the team is lost. As a result, their teams will lose enthusiasm and become less effective. In our case, the volunteer committee would likely have become apathetic and resigned. Fortunately, we had an atmosphere in which each of us felt free to express our individual *autonomous* opinions in the accepting environment of a group determined to reach a cooperative *consensus.*

For Feminine Energy *We* People to Develop Their Masculine Energy *Me*

Experiment with Independence If your Go-To Energy is Feminine in the *We/Me* Variable, you probably see yourself as the one who must work to ensure that others are happy. This can lead to dependency. Masculine Energy people have a more independent nature, which allows them to keep an objective, even detached, stance in relation to others in their lives. Experiment with identifying your own needs and ambitions, and make decisions based on your own well-being and self-interest instead of disappearing into the wishes of your boss, coworkers, partner, or children. This will increase your confidence.

For Masculine Energy *Me* People to Develop Their Feminine Energy *We*

Experiment with Reading Nonverbal Cues If your Go-To Energy is Masculine in the *We/Me* Variable, you will be a self-sufficient individual and will probably have very little interest in group discussions or decision-making. Those with Feminine Energy, who are very attuned to others, will interpret your disinterest as rejection. Pay attention to such coworkers by learning to read their nonverbal communication. Experiment by observing others' posture and facial expressions, and see what it tells you about how they are feeling. Then ask them about it. It will send a message that you care.

Chapter Four

Follow/Lead Variable

Leadership is not something you do to people.
It's something you do with people.

—*Ken Blanchard*

Characteristics of the Feminine Energy *Follow* and the Masculine Energy *Lead*

- In the *Follow* Variable, Feminine Energy is totally engaged and contributing, yet content to support the leader.
- In the *Lead* Variable, Masculine Energy wants to direct the action.

- In the *Follow* Vices, those with Feminine Energy submit to the point of being used.
- In the *Lead* Vices, those with Masculine Energy snuff out any outside contributions.

- When practicing Gender Physics and using both energies, people maintain their vision while being open to others' voices.

81

Typical Features of the Two Energies in This Variable

Feminine Energy: *Follow*	Masculine Energy: *Lead*
Genuinely interested in the other and accommodates idiosyncrasies	Very aware of position and assertively maintains it
Supports right of others to hold firm to beliefs and listens openly to understand them	Has strong opinions and enjoys explaining them to others
Is drawn to service and committed to a higher purpose	Organizes and directs the group's activities
Asks lots of questions to coax out the hopes and dreams of others	Finds it easy to establish boundaries and say "no"
Allows someone to go in front of them at the grocery store	Evaluates each action for the return it provides
Takes a back seat when others are making plans and never vies for position	Acts definitively and decisively during planning

Follow Is the Marching Band and *Lead* Is the Drum Major

Everyone loves a parade! The pomp! The showmanship! And out front, leading the whole spectacle—the drum major, ornately dressed, marching at the head of the band. Proudly *directing* what to play, when to play, and what tempo to keep are attributes of this skilled conductor. Using large gestures, signals, and whistles to *speak* to the group, the drum major stands erect with confident bearing and *assertively* sets the standard. Those who assume this position must like leadership, as they assume responsibility for *pushing* the band to deliver not only an impressive performance but also its best performance, every time. To achieve this success, they *establish boundaries* to ensure that the band is always marching and playing in formation.

To coordinate their music and drills, the band has its own set of responsibilities to fulfill. They *accommodate* the drum major by wearing their full uniform and ensuring that it is in good condition. Then they *allow* plenty of time for inspections. Aware that they need to know their stuff, they practice their music and drills, yet wait alertly for instructions. They assist the drum major in maintaining field discipline by *pulling* compliance out of other band members, and they adopt full *support* by *listening* for cues to play louder, softer, faster, or slower.

The drum major, leading the song—*pah oom pah pah, pah oom pah pah*—and a marching band, following their lead. The baton going up, coming down—precisely timed to each beat of the drum and mirrored by the cadence of shiny black shoes that ring out as they slap the pavement. The epitome of perfect team dynamics. The epitome of Gender Physics in action!

Follow and *Lead* Working Together with Gender Physics

Today, society places much more value on those who rise above and become leaders, but equally important are those called to service as followers. Leaders and followers do leadership together, so leading and following are both important skills. As Robert Kelley described in his *Harvard Business Review* article *"In Praise of Followers,"* many bosses don't have the skills to lead a horse to water, while many subordinates couldn't follow a parade. "Without his armies, after all, Napoleon was just a man with grandiose ambitions. Organizations stand or fall partly on the basis of how well their leaders lead, but partly also on the basis of how well their followers follow," he wrote.

Additionally, we want to become adept at both because as the old saying goes, it takes two to tango. My husband and I used to take ballroom dance lessons, but I felt it was sexist. Samba, waltz, and fox-trot—he always got to dictate the lead, and I had to react and follow. While he is musical and athletic, a natural free-form dancer, I can better remember the steps. Given my Masculine Energy, I wanted to lead but was relegated to following. This outdated idea left me very frustrated. That's why I loved the TED Talk given by Trevor Copp and Jeff Fox, who say dancing should be a negotiation, a partnership of equals. To support this theory, they developed a technique called "Liquid Lead," which aligns with my Gender Physics theory. Using both energies is an ongoing dance where one leads and the other follows and then it can change.

Gender Physics is a negotiated partnership of equals that flows like a dance

Getting to Know the Virtues, and Their Vices

In the *Follow/Lead* Variable, there is an overarching desire of Feminine Energy people to support the leader while those who prefer Masculine Energy like to direct the action. Each can be expressed by five related Virtues, which are strengths when used in appropriate amounts but, when used in absolute terms, can morph into Vices, or weaknesses.

Follow Virtues (Feminine Energy Strengths)	*Lead* Virtues (Masculine Energy Strengths)
Listen	Speak
Accommodate	Assert
Pull	Push
Support	Direct
Allow	Establish boundaries

Follow Virtues (Feminine Energy Strengths)	*Follow* Vices (Feminine Energy Weaknesses)
Listen	Cave in
Accommodate	Doormat
Pull	Absorb
Support	Placate
Allow	Submissive

Lead Virtues (Masculine Energy Strengths)	*Lead* Vices (Masculine Energy Weaknesses)
Speak	Monopolize
Assert	Aggressive
Push	Thwart
Direct	Dominate
Establish boundaries	Subjugate

Analyzing YOU

In Appendix 2, the Go-To Energy Evaluation, total your scores separately in each part for questions 6 to 10 (inclusive). If your score is higher in part 1, you operate from Feminine Energy *Follow* in this Variable. If your score is higher in part 2, your behavior is Masculine Energy *Lead* in this Variable.

Listen/Speak Virtues

Do you have a friend who calls and talks so much you could put down the phone and walk away and they would never know you were gone?

Virtue Feminine	Vice Feminine	Virtue Masculine	Vice Masculine
Listen	Cave in	Speak	Monopolize

Masculine Energy is *speaking*, projecting its ideas and using words to reach its goals. Feminine Energy is *listening*, which attracts others like a magnet draws iron filings. A good balance will allow you to give voice to your ideas while ensuring that you truly hear the positions of others. I wish I could tell you that I have always used a blending of both, but unfortunately that is not the case.

I once served on a board that represented a very fractured and polarized community. One side saw value in the organization and the other wanted it disbanded. Neither side gave the other even the slightest leeway. Any positive news released by the board was labeled as lies by the anti-organization group, while the group that favored the organization minimized any negative news and loudly cheered its successes. Both were so entrenched in their positions that all information was used to reinforce their existing belief systems. This tribal atmosphere meant that finding common ground was nearly impossible.

Since I was an independent board member, both groups wanted me to be on their side. They took turns lobbying hard to sway me to their way of thinking. Most days I was a pretty good listener, but on one particular day, I was not. Representatives from the anti-group had arrived at my office without an appointment on a particularly busy day. In spite of being tired and impatient with their continued antics, I agreed to see them and escorted them to the boardroom.

After listening for a short time to their one-sided recycled arguments, which I had heard many times before, I impetuously decided to let them know how childish and unproductive the bickering was. Speaking with the power of conviction, for several impassioned minutes I admonished them for their part in the organization's deadlock. They sat silent and eyes wide with obvious resentment. Although I knew it was useless and not a good idea, I carried on talking like a fundamentalist preacher, capitalizing on the opportunity to finally unload. Obviously, I had a lot of pent-up frustration because I concluded the meeting by telling them that I was busy and tired of them wasting my time. I'm not proud of this. Clearly, I was completely out of balance, acting with way too much Masculine Energy, *monopolizing* the meeting and losing any support that I had with this group.

I spoke too much and fell into the Masculine Energy Vice of monopolizing

They soon left, but that wasn't the end of it. Deciding that if I wasn't for them, I was against them, they then set out to destroy me. They started by writing an inflammatory letter to my company CEO saying that I was unprofessional and calling into question my personal ethics. It was hugely embarrassing to be in such a position, and I beat myself up pretty good for my impulsive antagonistic behavior.

Sheepishly, I reported the incident to the board of the polarized organization at the next meeting. Thankfully, they were very understanding. In hindsight, I can see that I wanted to openly listen to the complaints of the anti-group, but when I realized that anything short of totally acquiescing to their point of view wouldn't be acceptable, I lost it. I wasn't ready to fall into the Feminine Energy Vice of *caving in*. Instead, I swung too far the other way, *spoke* without *listening*, and fell into the Masculine Energy Vice of *monopolizing*.

As I demonstrated, those with an excess of Masculine Energy can be extremely intolerant of being interrupted and will try to push their ideas through by continuing to speak, even when people have stopped listening. On the Feminine Energy side, if we listen too much without forming our own opinions, we'll never find our own voice. A good conversation includes a healthy balance of both *listening* and *speaking*, where you express your opinion but are open to another's.

Listening is also a way of gathering information, while *speaking* is a way of convincing others to make change. Of course, the best result comes when action is taken based on listening. Ezra Klein wrote about this in an article he published on Hillary Clinton for Vox. He said that Clinton developed a comprehensive campaign plan to fight opiate addiction from comments on Post-it Notes she gathered during her 1999 Listening Tour. Every few weeks she would meet with her staff to organize the notes so that they could recognize correlations and areas of concern in order to address them. "Her way of dealing with the stories she hears is not just to repeat the story but to do something about the story," said her campaign chair, John Podesta. All of this demonstrates a good use of Gender Physics.

Accommodate/Assert Virtues

When your friends are seeing a film that is not to your taste, do you join them or meet up afterward?

Virtue Feminine	Vice Feminine	Virtue Masculine	Vice Masculine
Accommodate	Doormat	Assert	Aggressive

I walked down the hall at PotashCorp, beautiful rich carpet beneath my feet and gleaming oak wall panels on either side. Cradled in my arms was my recently created prototype of the company's sales manual. It was my first major project at PotashCorp, and I had thrown every ounce of my energy into it. I walked into the office of Don, our president of sales, handed over the manual, and advised him that I was prepared and ready to present.

"Oh, good," he said. "Thanks ... yeah ... we're looking forward to this. Oh, by the way, you won't be attending that meeting. We're going to have Gord present this project."

I felt like I'd been kicked in the gut. "What?" I sputtered. I could feel the anger rising in my chest but cautioned myself to take a deep breath and not react. "Gord knows nothing about the project," I said evenly. "It won't be nearly as successful without me there to explain it."

Don looked down, stammering excuses that were both vague and egregious. "Gord gives a good presentation ... men swear during these types of meetings and ... it's not an environment naturally suited for women ... You will hear things unfit for dainty ears," he said, in an unsuccessful attempt at humor. I didn't smile.

By accommo-dating others while asserting an opposing view, I used Gender Physics to reach my goal

I took another deep breath to compose myself. "I grew up above a bar in a small-town hotel," I replied coolly. "There is not a word out there that I haven't heard."

Reluctantly, he conceded that perhaps I could take care of myself during the meeting. But he continued to stall. And then changed tactics to argue that my presence would inhibit the men—specifically, their ability to swear and blow off steam.

I drew back my shoulders and stood tall. It was my presenta-tion and I intended to be the one giving it. I considered my options and knew that I needed to use Gender Physics tactics to reach my goal. I started by assuring Don that I respected his desire to have a successful meeting and that I always made every effort to *accommodate* his wishes. Then I *asserted* myself and said, "It really isn't acceptable to have someone else present my project, and I'm optimistic that you'll reconsider." With that, I drew a line in the sand with the hope that I had used enough Feminine Energy to keep from aggravating him in the process. I turned and left his office with as much authority as I could muster.

I hunted down my mentor and unleashed my frustration (probably a little too vehemently). While I hadn't been aggres-sive with Don, I'm afraid my mentor got the brunt of my wrath.

He wisely advised me to keep my emotions in check and assured me that he would lobby on my behalf. My efforts didn't end with him. I had a strong network of male friends at work, all of whom regularly went to sales meetings; I sought their offices next. I needed them to go to bat for me just as I would have done for them. If my voice was landing on Don's deaf ears, I would gather voices to speak up on my behalf. They all agreed.

Had I stayed in my Feminine Energy, I would have let my boss have his way. I would have moved from the Virtue of *accommodation* and into the Vice of being a *doormat*. I would have been nice (too nice) and helped Gord understand my program, in hopes that he would present it well at the sales meeting—because I wouldn't be there. However, while using my Masculine Energy to assert myself and defend my right to be there, I also had to be careful not to go too far ... not to dial it up to the extreme and fall into the Vice of becoming an *aggressor*. Because I left Don's office without demanding an immediate answer, I allowed him to make the decision, which then allowed him to save face.

Also of importance is the fact that *before* I needed it, I had used my Feminine Energy to establish a network of people that supported me. I had a mentor who championed me, and a group of colleagues who talked to their superiors about the situation. My network became the tipping point. Thus, collectively, we could circumnavigate an antiquated, old boys' policy and have it changed. I went on to attend that sales meeting ... as well as every sales meeting thereafter. It was simply assumed that I would be there, and women have been welcome at the sales meetings ever since. It was shifting between the energies that made this possible.

Pull/Push Virtues

Do you coax others into the swimming pool or get behind and push them in?

Virtue Feminine	Vice Feminine	Virtue Masculine	Vice Masculine
Pull	Absorb	Push	Thwart

A Feminine Energy person will *pull* information, attributes, and performance out of others, while Masculine Energy people will *push* out their thoughts, ideas, and way of doing things.

One day, back when PotashCorp had first gone public and we needed (but had difficulty getting) analyst coverage, I noticed that the share price of one of our competitors was moving when ours was not. Usually, every stock in the sector moves similarly, a kind of symmetry influenced by rumors such as China verging on a big potential order or Russia shutting down a mine. But on this day, one and *only* one of our competitors had a rising stock price.

I started poking around, asking questions. "Why is XYZ stock moving? What do people know that we don't?" After making a few calls, I was told that an analyst was out pounding the table to raise awareness about the benefits of our competitor. I realized that this analyst was not familiar with our company and was not covering us. *If he is following our competitor, it should be easy to get him to pick up coverage on us,* I thought. I made an appointment and went to see him.

He was a very flamboyant guy, his office populated with model train sets, toy trucks, and an array of gimmicky company giveaways. He had an umbrella stand crammed with faded pennants, and ball caps from various companies stapled to the walls and ceiling. His pants were too short, pulled high and belted over his belly, and he had these incredible eyebrows that looked like you could fly with them—big, bushy, and sprouting in different directions.

It was like meeting Santa Claus, but instead of being a jolly old guy, he was obviously tough and shrewd. Leaning back in his chair, he put me through my paces, knowledgeably asking questions or challenging each state-ment I made. I used Masculine Energy to confidently *push* back, giving him every statistic he needed. I also used my Feminine Energy to *pull* information from him and discover what mattered most to him, his hot buttons when recommending a stock. Then, I shifted back to Masculine Energy and addressed his concerns. Had I stayed too much in my Feminine Energy, I may have pulled too much information from him and become totally *absorbed.* Much the way a fever absorbs your strength, I could have given up my objectives, become lost in the information that I pulled from him, and weakened my position.

> Using Masculine Energy, I confidently pushed back, giving him every statistic he needed

Soon after our exchange, he began talking about our com-pany, and people began to pay attention. Investors started calling to ask, "Is it true that Brian Carlson is covering you?" After confirmation, they would say, "You know, I've made a lot of money with him before. I don't know anything about your company, but I'll buy your stock based solely on the fact that he recommends you."

He created the buzz we needed, we got the attention from investors that we sought, and our stock rose. It was a great start, but it wasn't always easy sailing. There were times when this analyst got overly enthusiastic and pushed our stock too hard. His unbalanced Masculine Energy was in danger of *thwarting* our progress. When he became overly aggressive and put out numbers that were wildly unrealistic, I would have to step in and *push* him to relax back. Throughout this relationship, I had to shift my energies from one gender to another as things changed and situations evolved. Fortunately, we had a symbiotic combination of *pushing* and *pulling* as we did the Gender Physics dance.

Support/Direct Virtues

Are you more comfortable behind the scenes as the sous chef or in front of the TV camera as the celebrity chef?

Virtue Feminine	Vice Feminine	Virtue Masculine	Vice Masculine
Support	Placate	Direct	Dominate

I remember sitting with a colleague at the boardroom table in our company offices waiting for our senior management to arrive. We barely acknowledged one another. Clutched tightly to our chests, we each held large boards with suggested advertising slogans for the sales department. Suddenly the door opened and three men came in. They briskly unbuttoned their suit jackets and sat down. I took a deep breath as the meeting began …

The week before, the two of us had been assigned the task of designing a new look for our company advertisements. To save money, instead of hiring an advertising agency, they had set up a competition (Masculine Energy) between my coworker and me to create a new slogan and campaign. We each took the project very seriously and used every minute of the time we'd been given to prepare for the presentation.

My colleague started with an idea that was much like something we had done before. It didn't feel fresh to me, and I could tell that management was less than enthusiastic as well. I then offered my slogan. I had thought long and hard about what our customers wanted from us and had arrived at the conclusion that it was responsiveness. I argued that no matter how good we were at mining and production, it was inevitable that occasionally there would be a hiccup and we would stub our toes. What was important, I argued, was that when we did, we would make it right. We would *support* customers in their businesses. If there was an issue with delivery time or product quality, our customers wanted to know that we would be there for them. Because we prided ourselves on doing a good job of exactly that, my ad theme was "We Respond."

Out-of-balance and one-sided relationships never last

I briefly explained this reasoning before presenting my idea and then stopped to measure their reaction. The suits looked doubtful. Finally, one of them said, "Responding is so passive."

"We want to show initiative," the other jumped in. "We need to be ahead of the pack. We want to *direct* the action, rather than play second fiddle. We don't want to acknowledge that we have problems."

Of course, thought my inside voice, *this is a Masculine Energy environment. We must always appear to be in total control with everyone else following our lead.* We prided ourselves on making the decisions and *directing* the action. I understood the desire of management not to completely cater to our customers and appease them at all costs. If we did that, the Virtue of *support* would fall into the Feminine Energy Vice of *placate*, where we would essentially give in to every demand no matter how unreasonable it was or how uncomfortable we felt. We weren't going to smooth over every conflict—we needed to stand our ground as well. After all, if we responded to every concern we'd never make any money!

As you can imagine, my idea didn't get to first base, but I did learn a lot from the experience. The results became more data for my experiments. Those who are operating with Masculine Energy tell others what it is and how it is. They always tout their abilities and never their possible shortcomings. They don't want to admit a weakness and they don't want to even the playing field. There are advantages to *directing*: initiating action gets you closer to your goals.

Results become data for your career experiment

Unfortunately, in their desire to always direct the action, they risk falling into the Vice of *domination,* where it is all about the company without consideration for the customer. Under this scenario, companies have their version of events and try to bully others into accepting them. Too many people think that the word *leadership* means having total authority, and this completely misses the point. You can only direct the action when you have people to support you. Out-of-balance and one-sided relationships never last.

We saw this unfold on October 5, 2017, when *The New Yorker* magazine rocked Hollywood with allegations against film mogul Harvey Weinstein. Female actors shared their stories of his harrowing sexual harassment, saying that he forced them to massage him and watch him naked. In return for these sexual favors, he promised to help advance their careers, but for those who didn't comply, there were repercussions. He retaliated and used his power to blacklist them and sabotage their careers. By October 10, allegations from thirteen more women were published in *The New Yorker*, including three accusations of rape. By October 12, *Vanity Fair* ran a list of sixty-three actresses and film-industry figures who cited the abuse they faced when interacting with Weinstein. Ultimately, he was fired from the company that bore his name; his wife and children left him; he was evicted from the organization behind the Academy Awards; and he was indicted. Weinstein wasn't a sex addict. He was in the extreme Vice of his Masculine Energy, using intimidation to prove his *dominant* position. While this went on for far too many years, true to Gender Physics, out-of-balance systems and people always fail, and his house of cards has come tumbling down.

Allow/Establish Boundaries Virtues

Do you insist that your dog sleep in its crate or does the dog rule?

Virtue Feminine	Vice Feminine	Virtue Masculine	Vice Masculine
Allow	Submissive	Establish boundaries	Subjugate

Allowing or establishing boundaries was illustrated at an informal dinner and discussion group that I held at my home. The evening was designed as an old-fashioned town hall meeting to gather grassroots support for mentoring women. Soon after the meal, a prominent businessman (who had accumulated a portfolio worth millions of dollars) said that the reason women didn't get further ahead in business was that they chose to put their careers on hold to have babies. The politically incorrect and unexpected comment seemed to come out of nowhere, ambushing the many women leaders present. Their easy chatter suddenly died and the room went silent.

One well-coiffed woman leaned forward out of the silence, looked him in the eye, and said with precision, "You should be glad that these smart, capable women are having babies. They're providing the future workforce for all your companies as well as the tax base to pay your old age pension in a few years."

The businessman smiled slightly, obviously comfortable with a little sparring. In fact, he was probably happy to be in his element and using his Masculine Energy to challenge and debate. I was delighted that one of my female guests had been so quick to step into her own Masculine Energy and *establish a boundary.*

I could tell by the collective body language that the rest of the women were ready to pounce on the businessman as well. But after pausing for a moment, he continued to talk, and they *allowed* him to carry on expressing his ideas. He told a story about when he had served on the board of a bank that did not have any women on it. The male board members would fly in from around the country, whiz through the meeting agenda, and by noon be enjoying a fancy lunch followed by fat cigars. He chuckled when describing how quickly they finished their meeting. He then went on to say that when the bank appointed some women to the board, they started asking questions and the length of the meetings doubled. With this comment, the women gathered in my dining room collectively stiffened and looked sideways at one another. Where was he going with this? Should they call him on these comments, be on guard for more insults? Was another, clearer boundary needed?

As the businessman continued to talk, it was as if a lightbulb went on: he started musing about what changed with women on the board. Yes, the meetings took longer, but soon the board was having better, more productive discussions and, ultimately, made better decisions for the company. There was more give and take, push and pull, with far better results. He concluded by saying that he had experienced the advantages women bring to an organization and whatever is needed to encourage them back to work after having babies should be done.

With that, the room visibly relaxed and discussion progressed. It was a great night, and before long, I was handing out coats and showing people to the door. The evening had been full of stimulating conversation and a great success, but looking back, I see the revelation of that businessman as the crowning moment.

> Masculine Energy creates the boundaries that drive an organization's culture

Boundaries at work are no different from the boundaries around your property. You decide what trees to plant and when to mow the grass. The leader in the office *establishes boundaries* to determine the standard of behavior and level of performance that is expected of the followers, and then the leader *allows* it to happen. During our discussion group, the women successfully used both energies. First, they used Masculine Energy to *establish a boundary* that it isn't okay to say that having a baby limits women's careers (even if he was just being provocative). Then, they used their Feminine Energy and *allowed* the businessman to express his true (and previously unexplored and unacknowledged) feelings that there is value for the system in encouraging women back to work after taking maternity leave.

Had the women not challenged the vocal businessman's negative comments about women thwarting their careers by having babies, they would have been *submissive*. By allowing themselves to be controlled by him and his opinions, they would have been in their Feminine Energy Vice. To their credit, these women didn't swing to their extreme opposite Vice and try to *subjugate* him to their point of view. If they had, each side would likely have dug in, and it could have resulted in a confrontation. Instead, they allowed the businessman to reconsider his experience in a new light with a different perspective. It can be tempting for leaders to bring others under the yoke of their control, but over the long term, they lose valuable input and enthusiasm from their followers by doing so. Fortunately, neither Vice arose, and the evening ended as a perfect example of the value of using both energies.

Feminine Energy people often defer to others to keep peace

For Feminine Energy *Follow* People to Develop Their Masculine Energy *Lead*

Experiment with Declarative Statements If your Go-To Energy is Feminine, you're apt to follow along and defer to the ideas of others simply to keep the peace. Masculine Energy people, who like to get out in front and lead, are not overly concerned about the impact of their needs and/or desires on others. Experiment with assertively expressing your opinion by making declarative statements. As Warren Beatty said in the film *Bonnie and Clyde,* "We rob banks." There was no doubt as to his occupation, and he came across as confident and sure of himself.

For Masculine Energy *Lead* People to Develop Their Feminine Energy *Follow*

Experiment with Giving Up Control If your Go-To Energy is Masculine, you likely consider conversation as a way to relay your information or gather information to help you reach your goals. Feminine Energy people, who are good listeners and often coax information out of others, can find you officious. Don't be insulted if others question you. Feminine Energy people will ask questions not just to clarify things but also to be sure that everyone is on the same page. They are not suggesting that you are incompetent. Experiment with giving up control by being open, slowing things down, and asking questions of others. This will send a message that you care.

Chapter Five

Build/Win Variable

Sometimes it is better to lose and do the right thing
than to win and do the wrong thing.

—*Tony Blair*

Characteristics of the Feminine Energy *Build* and the Masculine Energy *Win*

- In the *Build* Variable, Feminine Energy takes the time to put in place the things necessary to make progress.
- In the *Win* Variable, Masculine Energy focuses on getting better results faster than others.

- In the *Build* Vices, Feminine Energy despairs at the lengthy task and hopelessly gives up.
- In the *Win* Vices, Masculine Energy is interested only in securing first place, regardless of the cost.

- When practicing Gender Physics and using both energies, people earn the trust of end users while feeding their internal success barometer.

Typical Features of the Two Energies in This Variable

Feminine Energy: *Build*	Masculine Energy: *Win*
Places emphasis on egalitarian principles and building interpersonal relationships	Places emphasis on bettering self or corporate entity and believes it is all about the end result
Grows organizations organically over the long term	Has eye on the prize and wants results yesterday
Believes that a win-win offers better collaborative outcomes	Believes driving a win raises the bar of excellence for future outcomes
Invites others to meet at the same level	Sees oneself as being over or under others
Looks for nontraditional partners to accomplish things that would not be done alone	Likes to compete with colleagues to come out on top and gain status
Likes a decentralized organizational structure	Likes a centralized organizational structure
Is concerned about the business impact on the stakeholder	Is all about the financial bottom line
Shares information to build harmony with others	Uses information to create a pecking order
Avoids conflict	Sees life as a series of negotiations

Build Is the Tour de France and *Win* Is the Iron Man

Consider two different kinds of races: the Tour de France and the Iron Man. The Tour de France is a multi-day, multi-terrain race where success is achieved over the *long term* (*Build*). Rather than winning an individual lap, the team must *collaborate* to be awarded the title after the culmination of races over several days.

It cannot happen without *empowered* teamwork—teammates ride their bikes in a formation (*flat structure*) to cut down on the wind shear faced by their team leader. While there is one winner, it takes the backing of a team that can build *relationships* to make winning a reality.

An Iron Man competition (*Win*), on the other hand, is about the individual—there is no team. One person participates in three different marathons in one day (*short term*) with a goal of being first in the final *result*. The event consists of running, swimming, and cycling races, and participants must *compete* in all three regardless of their individual capabilities and strengths. To be a winner, one must exercise complete *command and control* over every aspect of the *competition*, since winning falls on them as an individual. The athlete that crosses the finish line first is granted the honor of standing on the winner's podium at the top of the *hierarchy*.

Build and *Win* Working Together with Gender Physics

Academy Award winner Natalie Portman gave us a perfect example of the *Build/Win* Variable during an onstage conversation at TIFF in 2015. She openly revealed that constructive criticism motivates her. When she performs in a scene and people gush, "Oh, that was great," her response is generally ho-hum. But when someone describes how she can construct and create a better performance and have greater impact on the audience, then she becomes alert and rises to the occasion. Through her ability to deftly shift between the energies, she achieved award-worthy status. Had she paid attention only to an Oscar *Win* rather than a best-performance *Build*, she may have missed the mark. Yet another reminder of the success that comes from using both energies with Gender Physics.

Getting to Know the Virtues, and Their Vices

In the *Build/Win* Variable there is an overarching desire of Feminine Energy people to make progress by building bonds, while those who prefer Masculine Energy want results fast (and especially faster than others). Each can be expressed by five related Virtues, which are strengths when used in appropriate amounts but, when used in absolute terms, can morph into Vices, or weaknesses.

Build Virtues (Feminine Energy Strengths)	*Win* Virtues (Masculine Energy Strengths)
Flat structure	Hierarchical structure
Collaboration	Competition
Relationships	Results
Long term	Short term
Empower	Command and control

Build Virtues (Feminine Energy Strengths)	*Build* Vices (Feminine Energy Weaknesses)
Flat structure	Confusion
Collaboration	Demoralized
Relationships	Needy
Long term	Disoriented
Empower	Enable

Win Virtues (Masculine Energy Strengths)	**Win Vices** (Masculine Energy Weaknesses)
Hierarchical structure	Dictatorship
Competition	Combative
Results	Oppressive
Short term	Addicted
Command and control	Overbearing

Analyzing YOU

In Appendix 2, the Go-To Energy Evaluation, total your scores separately in each part for questions 11 to 15 (inclusive). If your score is higher in part 1, you operate from Feminine Energy *Follow* in this Variable. If your score is higher in part 2, your behavior is Masculine Energy *Lead* in this Variable.

Flat Structure/Hierarchical Structure Virtues

What makes you think you are the boss of me?

Virtue Feminine	Vice Feminine	Virtue Masculine	Vice Masculine
Flat structure	Confusion	Hierarchical structure	Dictatorship

Most of us are familiar with the children's game "King of the Castle." In it, one child crawls to a higher point than the rest of the group and shrieks with glee, "I'm the king of the castle!" There they sit until another playmate climbs still higher and gets to claim the royal position. I have also observed similar behavior in a friend's Jack Russell Terrier, a breed known for its alpha tendencies. Regardless of gender, these dogs want to sit at the highest point in the room, and nothing less than being king (or queen) of the castle will do.

It's not only children and dogs that play this game. Business leaders around the globe vie for king-of-the-castle status by attempting to outbuild one another and claim the title of world's tallest building. This syndrome is a not-so-subtle display of Masculine Energy and stems from their need to categorize themselves in terms of being over or under others.

The hierarchy game is one that we play our whole lives. From an early age, we notice who is the tallest or the most athletic. This progresses to who's the smartest or who's making the most money. Even in a seniors' home, there is a hierarchy of sorts formed by who wins the most hands at bridge and who is in the best health. We tend to form hierarchies based on what is important to us at the time, and we then use those standards to determine what constitutes the top and who gets to sit there.

> The equality of access to information on the Internet is an example of Feminine Energy

While Masculine Energy is all about the *hierarchy*, Feminine Energy tends to look for equality among the members of a group, which creates a *flat structure*. This is one of the reasons that it's sometimes difficult for a person who infuses a lot of Feminine Energy in their interpersonal relationships to raise their head above the others. Like the story of crabs in a pot, when one tries to crawl out, the others pull them back down.

In 1993, *Time* magazine featured an article and the cover line "The Info Highway"—an early description of the Internet. When first reading it, I didn't quite grasp what a difference it was going to make in my life. At that time, much of the public information regarding potash consumption and production around the world emanated from my desk. One of my responsibilities was to interpret industry stats, compile the information for different audiences (offering different levels of complexity), and then distribute the reports. Context was important to people's understanding of the numbers, so I often laid the groundwork with a telephone conversation before faxing off a summary sheet. I was in the luxurious position of disseminating rather than reacting.

Soon after reading the article about the Information Highway, I experienced firsthand the impact it would have on business. At a one-on-one meeting in New York, an investor showed up with a six-inch stack of papers. Because it was our first interaction, and I hadn't faxed him any numbers, I was surprised by his depth of knowledge and taken aback when he immediately began quoting statistics and peppering me with questions. I later discovered that he was a new father who had taken paternity leave and had spent the time sitting in front of the computer with a baby son in the crook of his arm. Using this early version of the Internet, he had sent out questions to test each tenet of our strategy. He received back reams of facts, figures, and charts that he was anxious to discuss. That lively meeting was a game changer and a precursor of things to come.

> Masculine Energy will set up tribe-like mini-hierarchies

It was also an eye-opening interaction that left me smiling to myself with the realization that nothing in my world would ever be the same again. Up to that moment, it had been a hierarchical world where I distributed what I wanted, when I wanted. I knew that from that day forward I would be reacting to others. The Internet effectively created a flat organization where everyone had equal access to information.

Hierarchies are alive and well in the modern workplace, so it is important that we understand them. Often, they can feel a lot like a 3-D game of "Snakes and Ladders." The boss at the very top controls the game, and the more people under them, the more power they have to ensure that the game works to their advantage.

To move higher in the hierarchy, people have to 'power thump' one another. This means that any mistake made by another person is pointed out—"Look, they blew it and will take a slide, so I can move up!" The workplace can often be made up of tribe-like mini-hierarchies. These little kingdoms provide those in the group with protection from their common enemies. Members strive to promote the leader of their own group and make them superior to other leaders. Mistakes made by the leaders of another tribe are to be capitalized upon and/or publicly attacked so that their own leader can be promoted to the top of the pile.

Another move from the corporate gamesmanship manual is the 'power peck.' Once a member moves up the hierarchy, they peck others into place in order to solidify their newfound position. I once found myself being pecked into place when a colleague was promoted and I took over some of his previous duties. He wasted no time in telling me (in front of others) how to

change a program that until the day before had been his responsibility. Odd—the program was fine when he was handling it,
but now that he was my boss and the program fell under my
jurisdiction, suddenly it had to be revamped and reorganized.
He was power pecking me into my place below him. While he
talked, I nodded and concurred to show the appropriate respect
for his new authority. This acknowledged his higher place in the
hierarchy and reassured him that he would indeed receive my
loyalty in the future.

The key to success in any workplace structure is a combination
of both energies. That's why I found that the best antidote to the
hierarchy (and its accompanying power thump
and power peck) was to establish a base of my
own outside the company. This strategy
worked well when I made friends with the
gopher derby event organizers when I
worked at the brewery. It also worked well
with our customers when I was in sales and
with our investors when I was in head office. In
all cases, I created an external base of supporters
that was impossible for my colleagues internally to ignore. Once
again, I experimented with a balance of both energies.

> The best antidote to the hierarchy is to establish your own power base using Feminine Energy

When an organization is built only upon a Feminine Energy,
flat structure without some of its Complementary Masculine
Energy infused into it, the Vice is activated and the result can be
confusion about the objective or individual roles. With no one in
charge, it can become a place where no one makes any decisions
because they are afraid of offending someone.

When an organization that is stringently *hierarchical* falls
too far into Masculine Energy, it can begin to operate like a

dictatorship. The need to triumph at any cost can result in high body counts and the animosity of others. As Wilson Mizner put it in his well-known quote, "Be nice to people on your way up because you'll meet them on your way down." People who must win at the expense of others eventually learn this lesson.

Additionally, out-of-balance systems always topple. Some investors use a 'skyscraper index,' which says that aggressive building is often a negative leading indicator of an economic collapse. While some say the index is whimsical, the Shanghai Tower in China was officially crowned the second-tallest building in the world in January 2016, and on the same day, in direct correlation, the country's stock market had a major correction.

Collaboration/Competition Virtues

Does the person next to you have your back or should you be watching your back?

Virtue Feminine	Vice Feminine	Virtue Masculine	Vice Masculine
Collaboration	Demoralized	Competition	Combative

Competition is Masculine Energy. Companies that take a discovery to market before their competition are rewarded with recognition and greater earnings. Likewise, competitive individuals in the workplace can push one another to greater heights, benefiting the company as a whole. We can credit competition with inspiring people to improve education and health care and sending people to the moon.

The importance of this was demonstrated in the 2016 film *Hidden Figures,* which was based on the early years of the US space program. A successful Soviet rocket launch during the

Cold War spurred the competitive spirit of the American government, which, in turn, put pressure on NASA to outperform the Russians. To surpass them, NASA had to put forth their best talent, which provided three African-American women mathematicians an opportunity to serve in vital roles. Even though the white male scientists at NASA were not initially welcoming, their desire to beat the Russians meant that the women were eventually included.

Collaboration is Feminine Energy, and we are seeing its successful use with the advent of the sharing economy. Matching underused assets with needs is the basis of the successful Airbnb and Uber business models. Both depend upon on people's willingness to collaborate. Sometimes even competitors in the marketplace collaborate for the greater good of both. For example, in March 2018, BMW and Toyota introduced a next-generation sports car to replace the former's aging Z4 and the latter's Supra. By overcoming cutthroat competitive attitudes, they collaborated to produce a better and more marketable product.

When working at PotashCorp, I was part of many acquisitions. However, one was particularly difficult since the company we purchased didn't want to collaborate. Their previous owners, a company owned by the French government, had been very hands-off and given them lots of autonomy. Suddenly their comfortable modus operandi of large departments, big budgets, and little accountability was replaced with smaller departments, greater oversight, and budgets based upon results. Their resentment with the new culture was palpable. It was especially difficult for me because our new employees were from the Southern US, and these very traditional men resented having to report to a woman.

Phone calls to newly acquired employees who reported to me were often not returned. When they were, responses to questions consisted of terse one-word answers. Using my Feminine Energy—I tried to 'tend and befriend' them by taking them out for a nice dinner—didn't get me very far. The evening was an uncomfortable flop. Clearly, they viewed me as *competition*. I wasn't the only one having trouble, so our CEO organized a meeting between our two organizations in an attempt to establish better understanding and find common ground.

A few days before departing for the meeting, a friend and colleague dropped by my office to stress the urgency of the situation. He pointed out that the current work balance between our company and the one we acquired was precariously lopsided and communication was dismal. "If you're not careful," he said, "they'll sneak up from behind and do a reverse takeover of your department. You need to use this meeting to set the record straight. Be strong; make it clear you're the boss, not them. It's time to take them out behind the woodshed."

Feminine Energy is prone to tend and befriend

When it came time for me to speak at the management meeting, I found myself at the podium facing one hundred men. Everyone from management to the CEOs—from both companies—stared up at me. I could feel as well as see smirking, smug glances being blatantly exchanged amongst those from the acquired company. Realizing the gravity of what was at stake, I felt nervous and uncertain. And though my knees were knocking, I knew it was time to dive in. So I took a deep breath, resolutely squared my shoulders, and steadily returned their gaze from the front of the room.

In no uncertain terms, I explained it to them in a way that could not be misunderstood. I told them what and how things were going to be done and broached what, moving forward, was going to be the "zero room for disparity or dissension amongst our group policy." I demanded transparency and cooperation. Gradually, as I spoke, my resolve strengthened, and by the time I reached the conclusion, I was fully self-possessed. I reminded the group that starting now, there would be ramifications if our policy wasn't followed.

The head of the newly acquired company looked at my CEO, nodded, and then gave the thumbs-up. Whatever his personal feelings might have been, he intended to get behind and follow this directive. Given his obvious support, one by one his managers (who previously had given me such a rough time) shrugged and begrudgingly nodded their approval as well. The woodshed approach really worked, and following that meeting, I am happy to tell you that things progressed smoothly between the new members of my department and me.

> By giving up limiting stereotypes, we can choose the best energy for every situation

My natural inclination to deal with the situation by leading with Feminine Energy simply wasn't suitable or effective. If it hadn't been for the sage advice of my friend, I may have remained spinning my wheels in my Feminine Energy. When he said, "You can't make friends with everyone," it was a huge moment for me. I knew I needed to shift into my Masculine Energy and take a stand. I had to win the competition for power with them by using the superior position of my CEO over theirs, and it worked. From that point on, I then used Feminine Energy to develop good personal relationships with our newly acquired employees. In fact, once we got past the internal *competition* and started *collaborating* and taking on the true competition—the other companies in the marketplace—we turned out a lot of good work together.

When you fall too far into your Feminine Energy, *collaboration* becomes *demoralizing*. Often, you end up with too many people vying to have their opinion heard, and when they are overlooked, they become discouraged and feel diminished. Collaboration is only successful when all concerned have something to bring to the party and are willing to contribute, and everyone is open to other opinions. When I was trying to collaborate with the employees of our new acquisition and they weren't interested, I was putting forth more effort and resources, and the relationship was out of balance.

If you fall too far over into the Masculine Energy Vice of *competition*, there is the danger that you'll become *combative* and view everyone as the enemy. When in this Vice, company employees will operate in silos, viewing others who should be on their team as the opposition. There is typically a lot of backbiting and internal conflict. It becomes a dog-eat-dog environment with unhealthy rivalries that result in workers resenting one another and creating unnecessary stress, which is counterproductive. Additionally, a combative win-at-all-costs attitude will encourage unethical practices, which can harm relationships and, ultimately, the organization's reputation.

We see this in Donald Trump, the current president of the United States, who views life as a competition, whether it is for money, status, or media coverage. In this Vice, he takes everything personally, feeling that everyone is out to get him and that no one is paying him the respect he deserves. He complains that the system is rigged against him, the courts are unfair to him, the media is lying about him, and the intelligence agencies are lined up against him. Thus, he *combatively* attacks companies and individuals with his tweets.

The beauty is that you do not have to enter the territory of either Vice, as both energies are present in you and available to use. You don't have to *collaborate* on minutiae (such as which brand of photocopier paper to buy), but on large complex problems, using all the skills of many people can garner superior results. That's probably why Nobel prizes are increasingly awarded to teams rather than to individuals. In the first half of the twentieth century, 90 percent of the Nobel prizes in the physical sciences went to people working alone; after 1950, half of the prizes went to teams and half to individuals.

Relationships/Results Virtues

Ever been the first to order your food and yet the last to eat because you took so much time making new friends at the surrounding tables?

Virtue Feminine	Vice Feminine	Virtue Masculine	Vice Masculine
Relationships	Needy	Results	Oppressive

Building *relationships* is Feminine Energy while going for *results* is Masculine Energy. We live in a society that treasures results and equates them with leadership, and yet most results are dependent on the building of a relationship first. The importance of this was something that I learned when PotashCorp became a public company in 1989 and I assumed responsibility for investor relations.

The biggest challenge of my newly appointed position was obtaining analyst coverage for our stock—a difficult task, considering fertilizer markets were stagnant without a glimmer of hope on the horizon. Brokerage companies employ analysts to recommend whether an investor should buy or sell shares, and the analysts' pay depends on commissions earned from the resulting trades. The fact that our company was out of favor was evident from the low levels of daily trading (liquidity), which left analysts understandably ambivalent about our stock.

Pursuing analysts was a frustrating business. My pitching the benefits of our company—good reserves and low-cost production; its value for growing world markets; the excellent long-term outlook—fell on deaf ears. There was little variation in their responses, which typically went: "It's a big investment of my time to write a report and you guys have no liquidity, so I won't get a return on my investment." I mused on the irony of this chicken-or-egg situation: our company wasn't trading because the analysts weren't writing—yet the analysts weren't writing because the company wasn't trading.

One day, I visited a very solid analyst in New York named Moe and gave him my spiel. Not surprisingly, my request for coverage ended with the same token response I had gotten from every other analyst I'd spoken to. Though fatigued and discouraged, I could see that going for results wasn't working. I had to change energies if I was to persuade him to reconsider and break the logjam of inactivity.

Suddenly, an image of his boss appeared in my mind. Moe's boss was a short, eccentric man, ostentatious in both dress and personality. Moe, on the other hand, was a safe dresser: conservative brown suit, cream shirt with a brown-and-cream striped tie. On the rare occasion that he did step out, I suspected that it would probably be in a gray suit with a gray striped tie.

I pointed out this observation to him. "C'mon, Moe, look at yourself. Your boss has a handlebar mustache. He wears suspenders and novelty ties covered in stock market symbols. He knows how to take a risk, and here you are, wearing brown from head to toe. It's time to step out of your comfort zone. That's it! I'm making it my job to find you some flamboyant ties. When you are ready to wear one, you'll be ready to cover our company."

Moe chuckled but remained unmoved by my appeal. I didn't give up on him, though. In that era, novelty ties were having their moment. Everywhere you looked, men were wearing figurative ties covered in cartoon characters such as Mickey Mouse golfing or Sylvester shooting hoops. I found an electric-blue tie covered in bright-yellow corncobs and mailed it to him with a note reminding him that corn is a very important food staple around the world and potash is important in its production. Later, I sent another one sprinkled with little tractors and a note saying that every solid economy in the world is predicated on a strong agricultural economy. This depends on potash application, so it can't be ignored.

Using Feminine Energy, I formed a relationship to reach my desired Masculine Energy result

I regularly phoned him to discuss market conditions and would always inquire about his tie. "What kind of tie are you wearing today, Moe?" I could sense his sheepish grin through the phone.

"You know me, Betty-Ann. It's a boring one."

I would always end our calls by saying, "One of these days, Moe, you'll be ready to step outside of your comfort zone, take a risk, and wear one of those ties—and then I'll know that you're ready to cover our company."

One day, while I was speaking with a small group following a presentation in New York, Moe joined us wearing one of the ties I had sent him. "Moe," I laughed, "good work!" I summoned a few other people to show them. "Look at Moe's tie. He's really stepping out!"

Of course, he blushed at the attention but grinned widely and said, "I just put out a buy in your company." I was elated.

A few years later, I was nominated as the top investor relations person in Canada. Moe wrote a letter of support, stating that my ability to form relationships increased the value of the company. It was a shining moment for me. No higher praise can be given to someone in investor relations.

> The Vice of oppression comes from overattachment to the Masculine Energy desire for results

Had I stayed solely in Masculine Energy and focused only on my end goal, I may never have gained Moe's endorsement and the coverage so important for PotashCorp. His models worked and when he made a buy recommendation, people paid attention.

Conversely, if I had stayed only in my Feminine Energy, I might never have pushed for his coverage to begin with—or perhaps never have found the nerve to call on him. It likely would have felt safer to stay in my office and wait for someone to come to me and offer the coverage … though my phone was silent on that front.

Using too much of either energy would have resulted in turning these Virtues into Vices. Too much Masculine Energy focused on *results* and you become *oppressive*—someone who is only interested in the win. I could have *oppressively* smothered Moe with demands for coverage or *oppressively* driven myself, knocking on doors until my knuckles bled. Fortunately, I dialed it down and focused on *relationship*.

An excess of Feminine Energy can create the Vice of becoming *needy*, where no matter how good the relationship, it isn't enough. With the lack of coverage from the investment community, I could have twisted myself into a pretzel repositioning our story and trying to gain approval. Being overly concerned about these relationships would have been so one-sided that it would have been dysfunctional. It was far better for me to balance my *relationships* with *results*.

An excess of Feminine Energy can create the Vice of becoming needy

My experience with Moe is an example of Gender Physics at work. By using my Feminine Energy, I invested time in establishing a rapport and relationship with him. However, equally important was that I also cultivated my Masculine Energy by making it clear that I wanted to garner coverage of our company. Using both these energies not only provided me with the outcome I was aiming for but also rewarded me with a trusted friend and business contact. Moe and I still exchange yearly Christmas cards.

Long Term/Short Term Virtues

Do you hold out to buy the house that you really want or settle for something you'll sell next season?

Virtue Feminine	Vice Feminine	Virtue Masculine	Vice Masculine
Long term	Disoriented	Short term	Addicted

It took a CEO with an innate sense of Gender Physics to teach me the value of not competitively rushing into action but instead leaning back and adopting a *long-term* strategy, the essence of Feminine Energy. I remember him coming into my office in late 1990 and sitting half-perched on my oak credenza. I could tell by the serious look on his face that the topic was an important one, and I put down my pen to listen.

He crossed his arms, pursed his lips, and began to describe the serious situation that had developed with potash exports from Russia. The centralized government of the USSR had traditionally kept their potash for internal use behind the Iron Curtain. With perestroika (the political movement for reformation within the Communist Party of the Soviet Union), their mines were now allowed to export anything produced over and above their internal consumption requirements.

This potash was making its way into world markets, and we were facing the occasional USSR ship offering to sell its potash contents to customers that we considered 'ours.' When one of these rogue USSR ships arrived in a country, the customers there would call and advise us that the USSR was undercutting our prices. They would offer to continue buying from us—if we would lower our price. The CEO wanted me to be aware of our position in case the investment community called with questions: we were not going to match the lower prices.

"XYZ is our customer and an important part of our market share ... how could we let them buy from the Russians?" I gasped. With a slight smile at my passionate outburst, my CEO patiently explained our strategy. As soon as a ship full of potash left the harbor in the USSR, it was not going back until it was empty. If we matched the price for the first customer, the ship would just offer the lower price to a different customer. Then we would be forced to respond to that customer by again lowering our price. Potentially, instead of losing one customer to a lower price, we would undercut ourselves multiple times, losing much more financially than we would by simply ignoring the USSR from the outset.

When faced with similar circumstances, many people would have reacted to the *short-term* problem in isolation. They would have immediately jumped in to protect their market share—action is Masculine Energy. Instead, my CEO chose a wide-angle lens to look at the big picture and see how a move now might impact the future. He then worked backwards and determined that it was better to take the *long-term* view and wait it out. His wisdom and logic were undeniable.

> Use Masculine Energy to capitalize on immediate opportunities

While this CEO definitely had Masculine Go-To Energy, he adeptly shifted and used a Feminine Energy strategy. He analyzed his strategy like a chess master, not making a move until he had reasoned through every possible and probable move of opponents all the way to the end game. In the moment, a skilled chess player may sacrifice a queen, less concerned about the short-term danger of losing it than about the cost of keeping it and what that will mean for the following moves and overall strategy.

Conversely, those who spend too much time on the *long term* without considering the *short term* are in danger of becoming *disoriented*, as nothing has meaning or context. People struggling within this Vice can miss immediate experiences with their friends and loved ones because they are so engrossed with next week's (or month's) business—they forget to live in the present.

Considering only the *short term* can provide immediate gratification, but when there is too much Masculine Energy in play, and it isn't balanced with consideration for the *long term*, it can lead to irresponsible actions. (Think of a chipmunk that neglects to store nuts for the winter.) Being overly engrossed in the immediate short term can result in the Vice of *addiction*. Those who act impetuously or seek the adrenaline rush of one short-term action after another can end up in a constant and unhealthy fight-or-flight mode.

A Feminine Energy strategy takes a wide-angle lens and looks at the long term

It is crucial to remember that *short-term* decisions affect the *long-term* livelihood of the business, and the two are inexorably intertwined. One never operates in isolation from the other. In fact, it is best if all *short-term* decisions are made within the context of a *long-term* plan. When they are worked together using the benefits of Gender Physics, the company has the opportunity to truly flourish.

Empowerment/Command and Control Virtues

When the boss tells you which wine to drink, do you comply or order a cocktail instead?

Virtue Feminine	Vice Feminine	Virtue Masculine	Vice Masculine
Empower	Enable	Command and control	Overbearing

When I was in high school, my history teacher captivated me with his explanation of a benevolent dictator, describing them as individuals who have ultimate authority but act in the best wishes of their constituents. While many dictators claim to care about their people, some are camouflaging a thirst for power, which disables their constituents. It is often hard to determine which one is which.

Paul Kagame, the president of Rwanda, has led the country since the end of their terrible genocide in 1994 and has been credited with the recovery and reformation of Rwanda. The country stands head and shoulders above other African nations, relatively free of corruption, remaining stable and safe in a precarious region. I view him as a benevolent dictator, since he has been exercising tight *command and control* over the country's media while *empowering* many women in his government. The country's constitution, passed in 2003, decreed that 30 percent of parliamentary seats be reserved for women, and in 2017 they comprised 61 percent of the lower house of parliament and 38 percent of the upper house.

I've traveled to Rwanda and have seen how much the people revere and respect Kagame. A young man we befriended there described the increased confidence of the country's residents since embracing their leader's vision that they become self-reliant, not requiring international aid. His impassioned description of what he hoped for in his country reminded me of what Stephen Covey observed in his book *The 7 Habits of Highly Effective People.* Covey described an empowered organization as one where individuals have the skills, desire, and opportunity to succeed in a way that advances the organization.

In this case, it would be a country. However, in spite of Kagame's inspiration, he is widely criticized in the West where many believe that he has taken the power of his position too far by limiting free speech and acting outside of international law. One day, I hope we will look back on history and see him as being a good example of the successful blending of *command, control,* and *empowerment.*

> There is a fine line between Masculine Energy controlling and Feminine Energy empowering

There is a fine line between *controlling* and *empowering.* Just as my father had to gauge when to release his steadying hold on my bike so I could learn to ride on my own, leaders, too, need to know when to step back and let go.

When PotashCorp went public, I remember stepping off the elevator on the executive floor the first day after being named vice president with responsibility for investor relations. It was a heady moment, and I felt like I had finally arrived. Opening the door to my new office, I stepped in and was happily overwhelmed by the rich oak paneling, elegant furnishings, and large corner window. However, the elation was short lived. In the background was the incessant ringing of the phone as my secretary frantically took one message after another from people demanding my immediate attention.

Our share price was dropping quickly. Those who had purchased our initial public offering were losing money and demanding an explanation. I attempted some semblance of order by sorting my fistful of messages by priority. This did not work very well because all of them were marked "urgent." I panicked, feeling very unprepared for this onslaught. While I understood the business of potash, I didn't have a financial background, but the angry people on the other end of the phone were not about to grant me any leeway because of my greenness.

My stomach was in knots as I started making calls. I was partway into dialing a number when a tall, expensively dressed, supremely composed man entered my office. He was our Toronto legal counsel, and he ordered me to hang up immediately and cease speaking to investors. "But I've just been made a vice president with responsibility for investor relations," I told him. "It's my job to talk to people."

By using Masculine Energy self-talk I gained Feminine Energy empowerment

He wasn't swayed. "Your share price is going down. People who have lost money will want somebody to blame; they could easily band together and bring a class-action lawsuit against the company. You could find yourself on the witness stand where anything you say can, and will, be used against you. Are they paying you enough money to risk going to jail?"

He had certainly made himself clear. I carefully replaced the receiver, and he left my office satisfied that he had made his point. All of two minutes passed before the vice president of mergers and acquisitions came to the doorway of my office: "Who are you going to talk to first and what will you say?" I told him about the stern warning I had just received from the man I somewhat sarcastically called our 'outhouse' legal counsel, but he seemed undaunted. He simply shook his head. "Our share price is our currency; we have to increase its value to grow the company. You need to ignore what he said and carry on. Do your job," he said bluntly.

I sat immobile for a moment, unable to identify my next step. Pick up the phone? Ignore the phone? I was the new kid on the block and had yet to establish credibility. I recalled the words of my CEO after making me VP: "None of us has been publicly traded before—it's up to you to figure it out. Just don't get into trouble." Now I was fully immersed in trouble. The knot in my stomach tightened.

Minutes later, a tall, swaggering salesman with a blinding smile and brilliant aura of self-confidence walked in to congratulate me on my new position. After thanking him, I realized he had something more to say. He paused for a moment before dropping the proverbial bombshell. "Betty-Ann, you need to lose weight."

I was stunned. The company was in a crisis and he felt it pertinent to discuss my appearance? "You're representing the company now, and you're not the image we want to present to the world," he stated, using his authority as heir apparent to the CEO. He added, "We want people to see us as a lean, mean fighting machine."

Whatever wind remained in my sails died. I felt anchorless, floundering, and defeated. Not only did I feel professionally incompetent, but apparently I was physically unacceptable as well. Convinced that nothing about me was right, I wanted nothing more than to crawl into a hole, or at least retreat to the safety of home, and leave this job far behind.

Silently, I rose from my chair and walked the sales executive out, closing the heavy door quietly behind him. Placing my back against the cool dark wood and looking back into the office that I had worked so hard to achieve, I stood in momentary despair. I'm not sure how long I remained there, paralyzed with doubt and indecision, but I do remember using some strong Masculine Energy self-talk to revitalize my spirit.

> By taking the Masculine Energy command and control leadership style too far, you can become overbearing

I would beat this. I resolved that I would tackle it the way I had tackled everything my whole life—head-on. Laying out the facts in my mind filled me with a determined calm. *I already knew the fertilizer business. I was a good communicator and knew how to market. I would teach myself the financial side of the business so I could effectively interact with the investment community.* With that, I picked up the phone and began to return calls.

Twice in the following few years, I was named the top investor relations person in Canada, first by my peers and then by my clients. I accepted those awards in the very 'fullness of my being.' Clearly, I had learned what was required of me. Looking back, I realize that the experience was about *empowering* myself on my own.

When our outhouse lawyer and the VP of mergers and acquisitions first came to see me, both were in their Masculine Energy, administering *command and control* leadership by instructing me what to do from their perspective. Obviously, they weren't ready to empower me.

The sales executive who came in and told me that I had to lose weight was in his Masculine Energy Vice and being *overbearing*. He wanted the quick win of walking in the door and looking oh-so-good! *Overbearing* bosses not only give unrealistic deadlines but also have unrealistic expectations, believing they can dictate how you should live your life. I can tell you from personal experience that it hurts employee morale.

In this case, my ability to personally *empower* myself saved the day for me as it increased my confidence and job satisfaction. However, if I had taken it too far, I would have fallen over into the Vice of becoming an *enabler*. With too much confidence from making my own decisions, I could have decided that I knew better than company management, stepped outside of company policy, and made my own rules. Then I would be prone to make excuses for my destructive behavior. If managers are going to empower their employees, they need to be aware that if they overextend this benefit, there are downsides. To operate effectively, we need to infuse our *empowerment* of others with some level of *command and control* to maintain company policies and systems. It takes both.

Activate your Masculine Energy and experiment with driving the agenda

As a footnote, my weight was never again a topic of discussion—as it shouldn't have been in the first place. Perhaps the heir apparent to the CEO could see (in my eyes) the inadvisability of ever bringing it up again (or perhaps he read reports of women like me winning discrimination lawsuits). He didn't know that it's no use having the sizzle without the steak.

For Feminine Energy *Build* People to Develop Their Masculine Energy *Win*

Experiment with Driving the Agenda If you are a Feminine Energy person in the *Build/Win* Variable, you probably lack the fire in your belly when negotiating and may be prone to giving in. Masculine Energy people who are used to getting what they want are not overly concerned about the impact of their needs and/or desires on others. Think about the result you want to achieve and experiment with driving the agenda. This may be uncomfortable at first because Feminine Energy people want to avoid conflict, but the more you rely on yourself, the easier it will be to take control and exert authority.

For Masculine Energy *Win* People to Develop Their Feminine Energy *Build*

Experiment with Giving In Those with Masculine Energy in the *Build/Win* Variable enjoy debate, like to win, and especially relish being right. They would rather make a point than make a friend. Those with Feminine Energy like to find common ground and often interpret the Masculine Energy communication style as a personal attack. Experiment by giving up your need to be right, acknowledge your contribution to hurt feelings, and offer up apologies more frequently.

Chapter Six

How/What Variable

If you're not sure where you are going,
you're liable to end up someplace else.

—Robert F. Mager

Characteristics of the Feminine Energy *How* and the Masculine Energy *What*

- In the *How* Variable, Feminine Energy relishes the process and considers all its aspects.

- In the *What* Variable, Masculine Energy lets detail fall away as it focuses on the goal.

- In the *How* Vices, those with Feminine Energy become overly involved in the exercise, losing sight of where they want to be.

- In the *What* Vices, those with Masculine Energy become so concerned with the outcome that they sacrifice integrity to achieve it.

- When practicing Gender Physics and using both energies, people remain cognizant of their mission while properly implementing processes.

133

Typical Features of the Two Energies in This Variable

Feminine Energy: *How*	Masculine Energy: *What*
Wants to see all parts, all at once	Wants to address one thing at a time
Jumps around, taking in all facets of an issue; prone to multitasking	Makes plans in a sequential and utilitarian manner
Interested in people	Interested in things
Works to live	Lives to work
Takes a circular approach to issues	Takes a very linear approach to issues
Loves taking time in the creative process	Is all about the desired end result
Wants contingency plans for potential upsets	Doesn't want to worry about things that might not happen
Prefers to gain as much information as possible and sees correlations	Prefers to compartmentalize

How Is Like Jazz Music and *What* Is Like Classical Music

There is a difference in focus between the *How* of Feminine Energy, which is oriented toward the mode in which a goal is reached, and the *What* of Masculine Energy, where the results take precedence over how they were achieved. Consider two different music styles, jazz and classical. Free-form jazz is more about the *process* of bringing the music into being. The musicians pride themselves on originality and often improvise rather than reading from sheet music. They are concerned with creating the mood or the feeling of the music. Someone in the *How* Variable will ensure that all the possible obstacles that might hinder the performance are provided for to *prevent problems*. Are the guitars tuned and the acoustics good? Jazz is a mentality; it's a way of approaching life, and it's about the *exercise* of jamming for hours without an agenda. Because it is enjoyed in the moment, its *stakeholders* most often prefer an informal setting. It is all about the *journey*.

On the other side of the metronome, the *goal* of classical musicians is that the notes on the page are played exactly as scored. For them, the *outcome* is about the structure and accuracy of the music. Certainly, a classical artist elicits an emotional response, but the *bottom line* is that the music is very much about hitting precise notes and rhythms at a specified time. To someone operating in the *What* Variable of the classical musician, the importance is in the culmination, the symphony. Their joy is derived from a worthy *destination*—the conquering of a challenging piece before an appreciative audience. They do not hold impromptu jam sessions but, rather, rehearse relentlessly, *resolving any problems* through practice. They hone their craft to a flawless end product.

How and *What* Working Together Using Gender Physics

John Kotter, the Konosuke Matsushita Professor of Leadership, Emeritus at Harvard Business School, wrote that management is about planning and controlling to get the appropriate systems in place, whereas leadership is about articulating a vision while anticipating and addressing change. His bottom line is that leadership is about knowing *What* to do while management is about knowing *How* to do it, and successful companies need both. The performance of companies, communities, and countries is enhanced by their balancing of energies by practicing Gender Physics.

There is probably no better example of the benefits that come from balancing the Feminine Energy of *How* and the Masculine Energy of *What* than the film *The Shawshank Redemption*. The story starts with an emotionally constipated banker, Andy Dufresne, played by Tim Robbins, being wrongly convicted of murdering his wife. After regular beatings by other prison inmates, he puts in place a process to help meet his larger future goals. First, he uses his financial skills to help the captain of the guard shelter tax on an inheritance, and then the warden uses him to manage the prison's financial matters, which leads to Andy laundering money for the warden. In the end, Andy escapes through a tunnel that took him nineteen years to dig with a rock hammer, withdraws the laundered money from banks, exposes the warden to the FBI, and crosses the border into Mexico. Watching Andy journey toward and subsequently reach his destination is not only fun and fulfilling but also a lesson: with proper attention to the setting up and exercising of step-by-step goals, we can achieve our desired outcome. And that's what Gender Physics is all about!

Getting to Know the Virtues, and Their Vices

In the *How/What* Variable, there is an overarching desire of Feminine Energy people to take in all parts of an issue while those who prefer Masculine Energy have a single-minded focus on the objective. Each can be expressed by five related Virtues, which are strengths when used in appropriate amounts but, when used in absolute terms, can morph into Vices, or weaknesses.

How Virtues (Feminine Energy Strengths)	*What* Virtues (Masculine Energy Strengths)
Process	Goal
Exercise	Outcome
Problem prevention	Problem resolution
Journey	Destination
Stakeholder	Bottom line

How Virtues (Feminine Energy Strengths)	*How* Vices (Feminine Energy Weaknesses)
Process	Overwhelm
Exercise	Exhaustion
Problem prevention	Paranoia
Journey	Procrastination
Stakeholder	Martyr

What Virtues (Masculine Energy Strengths)	*What* Vices (Masculine Energy Weaknesses)
Goal	Obsess
Outcome	Emptiness
Problem resolution	Quick fix
Destination	Impatience
Bottom line	Immoral

Analyzing YOU

In Appendix 2, the Go-To Energy Evaluation, total your scores separately in each part for questions 16 to 20 (inclusive). If your score is higher in part 1, you operate from Feminine Energy *How* in this Variable. If your score is higher in part 2, your behavior is Masculine Energy *What* in this Variable.

Process/Goal Virtues

"I want this relationship to be perfect before we get married" or "Okay, let's just get married and figure the rest out later."

Virtue Feminine	Vice Feminine	Virtue Masculine	Vice Masculine
Process	Overwhelm	Goal	Obsess

If you are a person whose Go-To Energy is Feminine and you are working in a Masculine Energy environment, you probably have to adopt a different *process* from that of your coworkers. The Feminine Energy inclination is to put your head down, focus on your work, and hope to be noticed, so inserting some Masculine Energy, which knows how to stand up and be recognized, will help you to reach your *goals*. I learned this firsthand while contemplating the arrival of a new company CEO.

Everyone knew that he was in the building and would be arriving shortly to meet the staff. There was a lot of nervous anticipation in the air. Suddenly, the elevator doors opened and he appeared. Handsome and impeccably dressed in a well-cut suit, our CEO cut an impressive figure. My male colleagues moved to greet him as if they were in a choreographed dance

I established a connection with my new boss by adhering to the same process. I didn't walk into his office and say, "Hi, I'm Betty-Ann, I'm valuable, and I deserve a promotion." That was obviously my *goal*, so there was some Masculine Energy at work there as well, but the *process* to get there was the key to my reaching my objective. First, I had to prove my value. Once again, you can see the importance of using both energies together to get the best possible result.

When I drafted that memo to the CEO, it took Masculine Energy to differentiate myself. It would have been easier for me to convince myself that if I did my work perfectly, that would be enough and that I would be noticed. That overemphasis on *process* would have been the worst of Gender Pull, as I likely would have been overlooked and would have ended up feeling angry and frustrated. When you dial this Feminine Energy Virtue up to the extreme, you end up being *overwhelmed* with the issues. This overemphasis on process will obstruct your vision of what actually must be done to reach your goal, and it comes at a time when you must be realistic. Like a child lost in the forest, you'll become increasingly uncertain, unable to clearly see the path to the goal.

Had I focused solely on my goal of being promoted, I would have leaned too far into Masculine Energy and risked igniting the Vice of *obsession*. Overmotivated, I would have tried too hard and become consumed with garnering the attention of my CEO. That would have made me an irritant rather than a valuable assistant. Had I been thinking constantly about my goal, I would have lost sight of the customer service that had made me successful in the first place. Instead, I experimented by pulling the strengths of both Virtues from the tool bag, and by using Gender Physics, I was rewarded with a promotion.

Exercise/Outcome Virtues

Are you content to fish for the sake of relaxation even if you don't catch anything?

Virtue Feminine	Vice Feminine	Virtue Masculine	Vice Masculine
Exercise	Exhaustion	Outcome	Emptiness

In the world of sports, coaches and managers realize the importance of both the *exercise* and the desired *outcome*, and there are many lessons that aspiring leaders can learn from them. First, there's the value of connecting with others, so necessary to building a cohesive team; then, there's using positive self-talk to enhance performance; and, finally, there is looking forward, rather than backward, when the opposition scores a goal. However, the most critical lesson that we can learn from great coaches—and one that is often overlooked—is to not *overexplain*.

When considering all the alternatives, we are in the Feminine Energy Virtue of doing the *exercise*—but we can get stuck there if we do not also take into consideration our desired *outcome*. That takes Masculine Energy. A scene in the baseball movie *Moneyball* demonstrates the use of both Masculine and Feminine Energy communication styles and the value of focusing on the *outcome* once we've been through the *exercise* and our decision has been made.

If the outcome is known, summon Masculine Energy and deliver the message with minimum explanation

In the film, Billy Beane (portrayed by Brad Pitt) teaches assistant general manager Peter Brand (Jonah Hill) how to tell a player he has been traded. "Don't give them fluff," he says, "just the facts." To strengthen his point, he asks, "Would you rather have a bullet to the head or five to the chest and bleed to death?"

Soon, the time comes when Brand must tell first baseman Carlos Peña that he has been traded. Remembering Bean's advice, he keeps it simple and gets straight to the point.

"That's all?" Peña then asks him. To which Brand replies, "Yes."

Peña answers, "Okay," and leaves the office. Brand watches him, semi-stunned at how painless it had been and how well it had worked. Then he breaks into a huge grin.

The beauty of this exchange is that the job was done using few words. Those who are in the *How* of Feminine Energy feel the need to fill in the space with a lot of explanation, which can end up being confusing. By the time they are finished justifying and defending, no one is quite sure of the message. Are they being traded or is there still an opportunity to stay? Bottom line: when there are fewer words spoken, there is less chance for misunderstanding. There is more clarity, more direct communication, and a greater chance the listener hears and comprehends what is being said.

> Feminine Energy uses communication to level the playing field

The natural and preferred communication style of Feminine Energy is to level the playing field. Rapport is built by apologizing, complimenting, and seeking approval. All of this opens the door to discussion and negotiation. This works well if we want to draw out the opinions of another or reach a consensus, but it is ineffective when delivering a predetermined message. When you already know the *outcome* (and especially if the news is going to hurt), an increase in verbiage doesn't improve the quality of the communication and it destabilizes your position. It is best to summon your Masculine Energy and deliver it with a minimum of explanation. When you know the *What,* keep it simple—you have more opportunity to control your message.

Very often, a lightbulb goes on for participants in my workshops when they realize the consequence of moving too quickly to reach a resolution without going through the exercise of properly considering the pros and cons. Without spending enough time on a task, they lose the gratification of having reached their goal and feel only the Masculine Energy Vice of *emptiness.* One young woman recounted how she was so focused on getting to Paris that she didn't spend any time planning and considering what she would do once she arrived there. She lost the joy of anticipation that comes with imagining all aspects of the trip in advance. Without any focus on the exercise, she arrived in the City of Lights and felt empty.

Conversely, those who forget the outcome and focus solely on the exercise fall into the Feminine Energy Vice of *exhaustion.* One young male workshop participant described an assignment in an engineering class where he had been asked to design a computer app. He spent so long on the task that he became completely *exhausted* considering all the possible permutations and entered the territory of diminishing returns. Had he infused more concern about the outcome into the equation, he would have had a more satisfying result—and probably gotten more sleep!

> Spending too much time on the exercise results in the Vice of exhaustion and diminishing returns

Problem Prevention/Problem Resolution Virtues

When going on vacation, do you plan your itinerary and book your planes, trains, and automobiles before you leave or do you wing it and figure things out along the way?

Virtue Feminine	Vice Feminine	Virtue Masculine	Vice Masculine
Problem prevention	Paranoia	Problem solution	Quick fix

Don stuck his head through the doorway of my office and unceremoniously blurted, "It's Barry's birthday—where is his cake?" He seemed in a hurry and distracted, as though the discussion was below him. Don was president of the company's sales division and had a rather inflated sense of self-importance. I could sympathize that he had lots on his mind, but was piqued that he was acting as if I had made a major blunder, as if arranging birthday cakes for everyone had suddenly become a part of my job description. Taken aback by this implication, my reaction was immediate.

"I have no idea when it's Barry's birthday as he doesn't report to me," I retorted somewhat sharply, as his head (along with the rest of him) carried on past my office. Inwardly, I thought, *Give me a break. I might get cakes for those in my own department, but I don't do it for the entire company.*

Just then Jean, our department's coordinator, gave a slight tap on my office door before stepping in with an amused look on her face. Cheerily, she announced that Don had stopped by her office as well, asking about a cake for Barry. Jean always seemed to look on the bright side of things, and her optimistic attitude instantly changed my demeanor. Suddenly, we were both laughing at the ludicrousness of it all.

The truth of the matter was we were a small department and our group was tight. We always acknowledged each other's birthdays with gifts and a cake. Typically, on someone's special day, we would invite the entire floor to the conference room, and after the birthday person blew out the candles, we would serve the cake for everyone to enjoy with afternoon coffee.

There were always lots of stories and jokes told, and a great time was the invariable result. Obviously, Don desired the same good camaraderie for the whole floor. That was *What* he wanted but had not stopped to focus on *How* it happened. Then, without thought or consultation, he had decided to add in-house birthday celebrations to my job description.

If he had thought it through and not acted in such haste, he would have realized that there was a better way to make the request. But he hadn't, and as a result, I considered the offhand remark fighting words. Full of Masculine Energy, I was ready to draw my boundaries and make a point immediately, and plainly. Of course, that would have been a mistake because, after all, he was my boss, even if he had acted a tiny bit like a chauvinist.

Too much focus on *What* we want without considering *How* it happens creates an imbalance

If I had taken this hasty action, I would have fallen into the Masculine Energy Vice of *quick fix*, which would not have advanced my career. I probably vacillated between both Vices, as I was also prone to the Feminine Energy Vice of being *paranoid* that all things domestic would be downloaded into my job description. I was going to prevent that from happening, no matter what it took.

Luckily, before I could march down the hall to straighten out Don, Jean said brightly, "From now on, let's have a monthly coffee party in honor of anyone who's had a birthday that month, regardless of which department they're from. We can have a communal cake celebration with the whole floor, and we can go out for lunch with the people from our department on their birthdays."

Fortunately for me that day, I had Jean working with me. She was such a nurturer, and she always looked for ways to build others up and *prevent problems* before they occurred.

Her solution was not only perfect but also a great example of utilizing both energies for success. Jean used Masculine Energy *problem resolution* to attend to the immediate issue at hand and Feminine Energy *problem prevention* (which supports the collective by finding a solution that suits everyone) to address future issues before they occurred. Three cheers for Jean and her adept use of Gender Physics!

Journey/Destination Virtues

When on a road trip, do you stop to look at the points of interest along the way?

Virtue Feminine	Vice Feminine	Virtue Masculine	Vice Masculine
Journey	Procrastination	Destination	Impatience

I learned the value of appreciating the journey rather than simply focusing on the destination during my first business trip after joining PotashCorp. I had been brought on under the 'you must hire a woman' policy, and the first day on the job, I overheard part of a conversation outside the office of my new boss.

"What are you going to do with her?"

"Simple. I'm going to send her down to travel with Wally. If she comes back, she can stay," I heard him reply.

Wally was something of a company celebrity. Not only was he the company's most successful salesperson, he was also a total character, and no one could predict what his next antic might be. His stellar sales record provided him with lots of latitude, and company management mostly looked the other way at his good-natured practical jokes.

So, after only two days at company headquarters, I found myself on a plane and on my way to the American Midwest to attend a momentous event for our company. The very first unit train (composed of railcars loaded entirely with potash) was due to arrive at a fancy new inland storage facility. Wally picked me up at the airport, and after introductions, we went directly to the train station to determine when the train would arrive. The stationmaster explained that unlike passenger trains, which adhere to a schedule, it could arrive as early as that evening, in the wee hours of the morning, or as late as the next day at noon.

With this information, we decided to check into our respective rooms at the motel before meeting some local fertilizer dealers for food and drinks in the motel's bar. One drink led to another, and with no end in sight, I feigned a trip to the washroom and headed to my room. After double-locking the door and readying a camera and film for photos to mark the train's arrival, I nestled into bed.

During the middle of the night, I woke to the startling noise of Wally banging on my door yelling, "Train's in! Train's in!" Hurriedly, I jumped out of bed, threw on clothes, grabbed my camera, and scrambling into my coat, ran for the car. Wally peeled out of the parking lot and we sped to the station. Once there, he swung into a spot and, after smacking the car into park and rummaging in the back, handed me a beer with a wide grin.

"Whoops, wrong train."

"Wrong train?" I said incredulously. Then it dawned on me ... "You got me up just to drink with you?" I laughed, shaking my head.

> With too much focus on the destination, you can miss the fun of the journey

"Yep!" he said, flashing the smile that had won a thousand contracts.

For the rest of that night and until the train arrived the next day, Wally shared stories and his vast knowledge of the company with me—the fertilizer market, its players, and our customer base. I could not have asked for a more insightful teacher, and through the years, the information served me well. I had been so focused on the *destination*—getting photos and a story about the arrival of the first train to exclusively transport potash—that I almost missed the opportunity to *journey* with (and learn from) the top salesman in the industry. Eventually, I did get the photos and story I needed, and today I count myself lucky to have been blessed with the opportunity of discovering early on (thanks to Wally's prank) the importance of balancing both the *journey* and the *destination*.

Those with Masculine Energy can be so focused on the destination that they fall over into the Vice of *impatience*. As it happens, this is one of my default Vices. My goal-oriented Masculine Energy means that I am prone to frustration when unexpected complications arise. I am also very time conscious; as a result, standing in slow-moving lines can leave me anxious and annoyed. That's when I have to remind myself to dial it back, take a deep breath, and smell the proverbial roses.

Those with Feminine Energy can get so enamored with the journey and where to stop along the way that they fall into the Vice of *procrastination*. They put off things they should be doing in favor of things that they want to do. We've all done it. When I was at university, I used to joke that the only time I cleaned out my dresser drawers was when I should have been studying for exams.

I freely admit to a burst of annoyed impatience with Wally for rousing me in the middle of the night, but fortunately, I shifted to the enjoyment of the journey and found some balance. Wally was a charming guy, but as luck would have it, I was focused on the destination—or it would have been easy to keep drinking and listening to his anecdotes, and I could have missed getting the pictures altogether!

Stakeholder/Bottom Line Virtues

If your waiter really listens to what you want, do you make sure that a big tip is added to the bill?

Virtue Feminine	Vice Feminine	Virtue Masculine	Vice Masculine
Stakeholder	Martyr	Bottom line	Immoral

In the late 1990s, it came to my attention that a growing body of investors believed that there was a correlation between companies that took care of their stakeholders and an improved bottom line. Thus, they were interested in more information than just the routine financials. They wanted to know how many toxins we were emitting into the environment, how safe our production plants were, how much we were donating to the community, and how we maintained relationships with our customers and suppliers. In short, they were interested in more than *What* the *bottom line* revealed; they wanted to know *How* we interfaced with our *stakeholders*.

As a company, we were doing many good things, and yet we weren't sharing our full story. The public was demanding transparency, and I concluded that we needed to be more proactive and produce a sustainability report. Additionally, we were a resource company that was eyeing acquisitions in other countries, many of which were in the early stages of development and didn't have good regulations themselves. How we conducted business in our home country was an important consideration for them when we sought approval for our acquisitions and a license to operate in their jurisdictions.

While I thought it was to our advantage to communicate this information to the public to enhance our reputation, many of my colleagues were opposed. Some didn't want the extra expense, some thought it was too time consuming, some didn't want the increased scrutiny and accountability, and others didn't consider it part of our mandate. Needless to say, it was more than an uphill battle finding support for the initiative.

Fortunately, I found a few individuals whose values were aligned with mine and who recognized the opportunity. We formed a committee with the objective of compiling a report. Many of the quantitative metrics that we were using internally, such as lost time accidents, emissions, and employee turnover, were already in existence, so it was simply a matter of our committing to be transparent and consistent with reporting the results. In addition to publishing those facts, the committee agreed that we would survey our stakeholders (employees, communities, customers, suppliers, and investors) each year to see how they perceived us and that we would publish those qualitative findings as well in the sustainability report.

As with most new (and relatively unpopular) initiatives, the first report was a challenge. There were more than a few days when the process was so messy and setting up a prototype was such a struggle that I questioned why I had taken it on. It became apparent that some of our information wasn't dependable and some was inconsistent. When I pushed for proof, I faced deep resentment and a dismissive attitude from my peers. They rolled their eyes, hoping that I would disappear so they could get on with their jobs. I felt like they were patting me on the head saying, "Let me tell you why this is more complicated than you can comprehend." However, I hung in, we got data we could stand behind, and we eventually completed the report. When it went on to win a national award, our CEO, who liked the recognition, got completely on board. With that, everyone else also fell in line (that's how the hierarchy works).

Company standards depend largely on the morality of the people who sit at the top of the hierarchy. Because their very livelihoods go up or down in direct relationship to the profits of the company, they can be tempted to look the other way when something is wrong and be inclined to omit asking the hard questions. These people may achieve outward monetary success, but blindly focusing on the *bottom line* at the expense of what is right will lead them into the Masculine Energy Vice of *immorality*.

> Balancing care of both the stakeholders and the bottom line demonstrates the value of Gender Physics

We witness this in the film *The Big Short*. Based on the true story of four outsiders (many called them greedy opportunists) who predicted the collapse of the 2008 housing market, the film shows how they made windfall profits by focusing on what the big banks, media, and government refused to see and acknowledge. While certainly bottom-line oriented, I'll leave it to you to decide if they fell into the Vice of *immorality*.

On the other side, when we focus too much on the *stakeholder*, we are in danger of falling into the Feminine Energy Vice of being a *martyr* and sacrificing too much for the cause. Joan of Arc, the fifteenth-century French war heroine, is probably the first name that comes to mind when we consider this Vice, but you don't have to be burned at the stake to qualify. A martyr at work can be the one who puts in long hours and makes sure that you know all about it. These people take great satisfaction in telling you all the sacrifices they are making in the name of servicing the company's stakeholders. Being the first to arrive at the office each morning and the last to leave each night might give them some perverse pleasure, but the reality of this behavior is that it isn't efficient or productive.

In our company's case, shifting between the *stakeholder* and the *bottom line* not only kept us from falling into either Vice but also turned out to be a huge advantage. Eventually, regulators made the measurements that we had adopted voluntarily a requirement in company reporting. Many of our competitors scrambled to institute metrics, but we could relax, as we were ahead of the curve, already having implemented them. Furthermore, it increased the number of ethical investors interested in purchasing our company's shares and made us more conscious of the results of our actions, which in the end yielded greater efficiencies. So the concern for the *stakeholder* actually improved our *bottom line* (and kept us in the limelight, winning awards).

Masculine Energy people will jump quickly to the end product

For Feminine Energy *How* People to Develop Their Masculine Energy *What*

Experiment with Breaking Down Big Goals into Little Goals If you are Feminine Energy in the *How/What* Variable, you probably love planning, and as soon as you get close to finalizing things, you retreat back to processing. Masculine Energy people, who have clear, focused intentions, have very little patience for the details of the process and will jump quickly to the end product. To foster better time management, experiment with setting small goals to keep yourself accountable. Begin with the end in mind and work backwards from where you need to be on a certain date to meet that goal. Then self-impose a boundary, such as, "We will have three options ready by Thursday, and on that day, we will decide which one we are going to present to our client." Putting this stake in the ground will give you confidence and assuage self-doubts about missing something. Furthermore, it will help you meet your deadlines.

For Masculine Energy *What* People to Develop Their Feminine Energy *How*

Experiment with Setting Up Systems Those who have a Go-To Masculine Energy in the *How/What* Variable are so focused on their goals that they don't take time to be sure that the proper systems, processes, and procedures are in place to help reach them. For example, I learned that it isn't enough to say, "I want to write a book." I had to allocate a day a week to putting 'seat in chair' and working on my manuscript. It's the same for runners who want to do a marathon. They must set a training schedule. If your Go-To Energy is Masculine, you'll have lots of goals, and your best way of reaching them is to use your Feminine Energy to establish a system. By writing (or running) each week, you'll establish a process to enable you to reach your objective.

Chapter Seven

Heart/Head Variable

*Our world requires that decisions be sourced and footnoted, and if we say
how we feel, we must also be prepared to elaborate on why we feel that way ...
We need to respect the fact that it is possible to know without knowing why
we know and accept that—sometimes—we're better off that way.*

—*Malcolm Gladwell*

Characteristics of the Feminine Energy *Heart* and the Masculine Energy *Head*

- In the *Heart* Variable, Feminine Energy is motivated by emotion and ideals.

- In the *Head* Variable, Masculine Energy seeks logical and reasoned examination.

- In the *Heart* Vices, Feminine Energy jumps wildly to unrealistic conclusions.

- In the *Head* Vices, Masculine Energy is heartless, over-thinks things, and is only interested in the obvious.

- When practicing Gender Physics and using both energies, people follow their hearts but take their heads with them.

Typical Features of the Two Energies in This Variable

Feminine Energy: *Heart*	Masculine Energy: *Head*
Sees connection between seemingly unrelated events	Likes data and works out solutions step by step
Enjoys esoteric philosophies	Only believes in things you can see, hear, or touch
Relates to people through shared emotions	Standards or rules are not up for debate
Goes with what feels right intuitively	Uses logic and order
Uses emotions to make sense of the world	Uses mechanistic decision-making
Feels others' feelings	Seeks solid reasons behind actions
Body centered	Thought centered
Relates to stories and metaphors	Convinced by facts
Relies on feelings to decide what to 'think' about things	Takes an impersonal, objective approach

Heart Is Like the Kindergarten Teacher and *Head* Is Like the Math Teacher

A good way to understand the *Heart/Head* Variable is to consider the core differences between a kindergarten teacher and a math teacher. A good kindergarten teacher (*Heart*) is very concerned about the health and welfare of the children in their class, knowing *intuitively* when one of the children needs something or hasn't had a good day.

Young children are establishing who they are, what they value and believe in, and it is their teacher and their parents who help them become who they really want to be. Kindergarten teachers help their students through *empathetic* nurturing and encouraging their *right brain* with stories and structured play. Kindergarten teachers operate from a heart-based place, using their Feminine Energy to help their students sift through their *feelings* and learn right from wrong.

In contrast, and especially when teaching higher grades, math teachers (*Head*) are very *left-brain* oriented. Their main goal is helping their students to solve mathematical computations that mostly have only one right answer. The math teacher is focused on *analysis* and *logic*, Masculine Energy activities that occur in the frontal lobe of the brain. This is the area of the brain where we *think*, make *rational* decisions, and synthesize information.

Clearly, these are overstated stereotypes because, in reality, the best teachers in any subject or grade are those who are concerned with the growth and development of their students as individuals as well as their students' mastery of the class material. Great teachers employ Gender Physics to infuse their lessons with both types of energies, most often simultaneously.

Heart and Head Working Together Using Gender Physics

In his book *A Whole New Mind: Why Right-Brainers Will Rule the Future*, Daniel Pink says the future belongs to people with androgynous minds—people who have analytical capability but also artistic, empathic ability. Although the military may be a macho profession, Pink says, in today's world, it requires a more sophisticated set of skills. Soldiers now need to be empathetic about the people of a certain region before they are released to do combat there. In other words, we need to use both our right and our left brain. In his own way, he is describing an entity whose Go-To Energy is Masculine, and he makes a compelling argument that it will get superior results by inserting Feminine Energy attributes into the mix.

This premise is reinforced by Dr. Paul Pearsall in his book *The Heart's Code: Tapping the Wisdom and Power of Our Heart Energy.* He wrote that society's dependence on the brain leaves too little room for the aptitude of the heart. The heart path represents a different way of interacting with the world than our current brain-dominant approach. He says that we'll benefit by being open to the flow of heart energy rather than always trying to master and control things.

> Feminine Energy people like to connect with others through their feelings

Getting to Know the Virtues, and Their Vices

In the *Head/Heart* Variable, there is an overarching desire of Feminine Energy people to connect with others through feelings and emotion while those who prefer Masculine Energy want logic and order. Each can be expressed by five related Virtues, which are strengths when used in appropriate amounts but, when used in absolute terms, can morph into Vices, or weaknesses.

Heart Virtue (Feminine Energy Strengths)	*Head* Virtue (Masculine Energy Strengths)
Intuition	Analysis
Emotion	Logic
Empathetic	Rational
Right brain	Left brain
Feeling	Thinking

Heart Virtues (Feminine Energy Strengths)	*Heart* Vices (Feminine Energy Weaknesses)
Intuition	Impulsiveness
Emotion	Overdramatic
Empathetic	People-pleaser
Right brain	Overstimulation
Feeling	Overreacting

Head Virtues (Masculine Energy Strengths)	*Head* Vices (Masculine Energy Weaknesses)
Analysis	Scrutiny
Logic	Rigid
Rational	Disdainful
Left brain	Compartmentalization
Thinking	Robotic

Analyzing YOU

In Appendix 2, the Go-To Energy Evaluation, total your scores separately in each part for questions 21 to 25 (inclusive). If your score is higher in part 1, you operate from Feminine Energy *Heart* in this Variable. If your score is higher in part 2, your behavior is Masculine Energy *Head* in this Variable.

Intuition/Analysis Virtues

Do you date someone with whom there is no chemistry because they receive a checkmark in every category on your spreadsheet?

Virtue Feminine	Vice Feminine	Virtue Masculine	Vice Masculine
Intuition	Impulsiveness	Analysis	Scrutiny

Within the first year of PotashCorp being publicly traded, market conditions deteriorated and the political party that had turned us from a government-owned company to a publicly traded one was replaced. The new party wished to roll back the clock and put us back under their jurisdiction. To add to all of this, there was a loophole that could make the new government's wishes a distinct possibility.

During that initial public offering, a number of shares were used to back bonds that were then sold to the people of Saskatchewan. The government was holding these shares in trust, and although the shares didn't technically belong to the government, it, nonetheless, had the ability to vote them. Recognizing that the newly appointed government was ideologically opposed to our status, I wanted to ensure that we would have enough shareholder support at our annual general meeting of shareholders to retain control.

After doing some research, I discovered that most institutional investors didn't bother to vote their shares; if they were unhappy with a company, they simply sold their shares and walked away. This revelation greatly concerned me. Should the government exercise the right to vote the shares backing the bonds at our annual meeting, and should we lack enough shares from the investment community to override them, we were at great risk. If this scenario materialized, theoretically, the government could get rid of the board and management, change our market-driven strategy, and, ultimately, hurt our value.

With this information, I approached our CEO and said, "I think we need to hire a proxy solicitor to ensure that we get all those votes in. If we don't, we may not have enough votes to control the meeting." He concurred. "Go do it," he told me.

I was the new vice president. When my colleagues discovered that I had employed a proxy-solicitation service, something they considered an unnecessary expense, they were annoyed and questioned my judgment. Everyone had suggestions for where the money would be better spent, and a couple suggested that I was fighting phantoms, foolishly and impetuously responding to an imaginary threat. Others scrutinized the situation and stated definitively that the government would never be that stupid since they would reduce the value of the bonds owned by their constituents. Hurting the pocketbook of their voters wasn't a good way to be reelected.

While their *analysis* made perfect sense, a flutter in the middle of my chest told me that there was a need to be concerned and I couldn't shake it. I could visualize a suit carrying a briefcase showing up and taking over our meeting, and I replied honestly to my critics: "My *intuition* is telling me that something isn't right, and I have to act on it."

The other executives sighed deeply as if I were a child who wasn't yet capable of understanding and shook their heads dismissively at me. This was hard to take, as I dearly wanted to fit in. But I summoned up my Masculine Energy and resolutely stood my ground.

On the day of the shareholders' meeting, a government representative did indeed arrive toting a briefcase filled with government votes, exactly as I had imagined. The government came prepared to overthrow our board. In fact, they had another board waiting in the wings—as well as a new management team standing on the sidelines. As to plan, however, we had enough votes to override theirs, and our company remained intact. I earned my credibility that day and am pleased to say that my fellow executives were big enough to come by my office after the meeting to say thanks.

> It was Feminine Energy that attached a loudspeaker to my intuition and forced me to pay attention

It was Feminine Energy that attached a loudspeaker to my *intuition* and forced me to pay attention. It was Masculine Energy that first spurred me to perform the *analysis,* then pushed me into action, and finally gave me the confidence to stand my ground. Both energies worked together to demonstrate the value of using Gender Physics.

Had I fallen into my Feminine Energy Vice and acted *impulsively,* I would have suggested hiring the proxy solicitor without doing the research, and the CEO would have most certainly turned me down. Fortunately, I had built my case for why it was important. It is also possible to do too much analysis and fall into the Masculine Energy Vice of *scrutiny*, where investigation and inspection denies the human element. When my colleagues were questioning my decision, discounting the power of intuition and calling it silly, they were demonstrating this Vice. I could understand their position, though, as it seemed totally illogical for the government to vote shares in a way that would hurt their constituents financially. Frankly, I would say that the government was out of balance, acting *impulsively* without having done their *analysis*.

Sometimes we will say things like, "Not sure how I know, but I know" or "I just have a feeling about it." That is our intuition speaking to us. Being a woman, my Gender Pull had encouraged me to use my intuition from a young age, so I was more open to accessing it than the guys I worked with. As you can see, by painting with both the big brush of *intuition* and the little brush of *analysis*, you can create a beautiful masterpiece. This balanced method is worthy of our trust and gratitude.

Emotion/Logic Virtues

When your friend tells you that it is silly to apologize because it won't be appreciated, do you still do it for your own peace of mind?

Virtue Feminine	Vice Feminine	Virtue Masculine	Vice Masculine
Emotion	Overdramatic	Logic	Rigid

I was on an investor tour in Europe, ending a busy day with a fancy meal with my boss. I remember walking into the glamorous, Michelin-recommended restaurant, imbued with a subtle and refined atmosphere. A faint glow from crystal chandeliers cast a warm illumination over the gilt frames of the paintings and the silken wallpaper with its intricate bird pattern. It was very different from the lingering memories of my childhood and the Royal Hotel in Strasbourg, Saskatchewan.

At some point during the main course, my boss said something very amusing and I responded accordingly, throwing back my head, opening my mouth, and giving a loud, hearty laugh. Suffice to say, it was not a titter; it was more like the kind of appreciative laughter I used to hear bellowing through the windows of the Strasbourg bar. But in this room, in this restaurant, people were taken aback, and as if on cue, they all turned as one and stared at me, aghast. Their pursed and polished faces held identical, almost baffled looks of vague distaste. Turning to my red-faced boss, I asked quietly if my laugh had embarrassed him. "It is pretty loud," he muttered under his breath. If you've heard the expression "like a fart in the room," you know exactly and completely how out of my element I felt.

> Balancing my Feminine Energy emotions with my Masculine Energy logic, I became my own best friend

While my laugh had been without pretense, a genuine response to external stimuli and an uninhibited expression of Feminine Energy, it was 'a little much' for the situation, venue, and audience. Later that evening, I had an emotional meltdown and fell into the Vice of being *overdramatic*. I castigated myself for my faux pas as I tossed and turned for hours in my hotel bed. *Was my laugh impeding my career? Should I try to mute it?* I was immersed in tremendous conflict. *Should I find a new job where I could better be myself? Should I stay with my current company and transfer to a different department? Maybe I should go back to sales where people laughed ... a lot.* That would get me out of my current executive position, and off what others referred to as 'the library floor.' There was certainly very little humor or laughter going on there.

By sunrise, I had made my decision: I loved to laugh; to give it up was far too great a price to pay. No, I chose to keep it and stay in my current position. Logically, I knew it was important to be my authentic self, and I knew they wouldn't fire me. I mentally ran through the personal foibles of the other executives and knew that my laugh was no more offensive than another's poor posture, pot belly, or crooked teeth. I concluded that more important than conforming to the expectations of someone else, my laughter was essential for my well-being. It was who I was at my core, and logically, I knew I couldn't deny myself that pleasure. Thanks to Gender Physics, I became my own best friend that night.

While emotions are instinctual they can be very powerful, so we must be careful to balance them with logic. If we don't, we will become *overdramatic* and that can harm our interactions in the world. Nobody wants to spend time with someone who is always upset, frustrated, sad, or anxious. However, we all have the ability to avoid this, and inserting some logic is the answer. However, if you use only *logic* without *emotion*, you'll fall too far into the Masculine Energy Vice of *rigidity*. When you are in this Vice, you are not able to bend or adapt, and you aren't interested in beliefs that can't be proven.

If I had chosen to give up my laugh, it would have been like putting on a straitjacket and giving up all ability to bask in the emotion of joy. Fortunately, I accepted my laugh and so did my workmates. My laugh became part of my signature. Whenever I returned from a vacation, colleagues would come by my office to tell me how much they had missed my laugh while I was away.

I chose my path by using Feminine Energy to guide me in following my *emotions* and counted on Masculine Energy to provide me with the *logic* to think it through. Masculine Energy also gave me the courage to embrace the attribute of differentiation. This signature hearty laugh of mine has served me well ever since and has helped teach me the importance of using both *logic* and *emotions* to make decisions.

Empathetic/Rational Virtues

When a friend is under the weather and describes their symptoms, do you feel them too?

Virtue Feminine	Vice Feminine	Virtue Masculine	Vice Masculine
Empathetic	People-pleaser	Rational	Disdainful

To walk a mile in someone else's shoes essentially means that before judging someone, you need to first understand their experiences and challenges. When you imagine yourself in their place, and see the world through their eyes, you are practicing empathy. Bob, one of the CEOs I once worked with, had a serious shortage of empathy for others, which resulted in him alienating one individual after another. As senior executives in the company, we used to joke amongst ourselves that "if Bob hasn't pissed them off, it could only be because he hasn't met them yet!" Consequently, we were always cleaning up after his encounters.

Unfortunately, he didn't see his inability to identify with others' feelings and emotions as a shortcoming. Instead, he viewed himself as someone who was totally *rational*, skilled at itemizing and weighing the pros and cons of every choice. What he didn't see in himself was the overall lack of respect he demonstrated toward others when their opinions and judgments didn't align with his. His lack of *empathy* meant that he spent a lot of time operating within the Vice of *disdain*, which seriously harmed his relationships.

I remember a specific incident when we were traveling to call on investors and were joined by another member of my department, a talented young woman named Cheryl. She had just returned to work after time off for maternity leave. My husband was also with us on that visit. The car trip was long and as the miles sped by, the four of us fell into discussion about our families ... Bob's four children, our two, and Cheryl's new baby. At some point, Cheryl mentioned how disappointed she had been that due to a medical condition, she had been unable to nurse her baby.

It was obvious to me that this was a painful topic for Cheryl and that she had a hard time coming to terms with what she considered to be her first 'failure' as a parent. Both my husband and I tried to reassure her that many children grow up to be healthy adults without this start. Our CEO, on the other hand, seemed oblivious to her self-condemnation. Instead, he chose to launch into a lecture regarding the many reasons why this was clearly a maternal shortcoming and how it would ultimately be detrimental to the baby. Relentlessly, he expounded on how his wife had insisted on breastfeeding to ensure that their children would have the best possible start in life. He went on ad nauseam, crowing about the health of his children ... how they were hardly ever sick ... had never developed allergies (certainly not asthma) ... all thanks to his wife's dedication and commitment to breastfeeding.

While Bob never explicitly said that Cheryl should have tried harder, the implication was clear, and his pontificating about the success of his wife's nursing only sharpened Cheryl's pain. I could see her wilt under the weight of his comments. A well-educated woman, she was well aware of the rationale of the evidence he was touting. Moreover, as her company superior, his words carried importance for her. She wanted him to think well of her, and I suspect she felt diminished as a mother and in the eyes of her boss.

> With too much empathy, the Feminine Energy Vice of people-pleasing becomes a danger

This CEO had reverted to "mansplaining," a term that has garnered a fair amount of media coverage recently. It's used to describe men who endeavor to explain the words or experiences of a woman to a woman. Generally, it entails a man speaking in a condescending manner about something of which he has little (or incomplete) knowledge and yet believes he knows more about the facts or situation than the woman he is addressing. Men—as well as women—who have power and platform and are too much in their Masculine Energy are prone to fall into this Vice.

Humour is often the smoothest way out. Seeing Cheryl's suffering, my husband, always the champion of the underdog, chimed in, saying to our CEO, "Bob, don't tell me that you're now an effing expert on breastfeeding too?" That broke the tension and everyone laughed.

Had our CEO chosen to insert a little *empathy* in his *rational* thinking, he could have gotten out of his Vice of *disdain* and also improved his relationship with the three of us. Unfortunately, he was sorely out of balance, and instead, we lost respect for him.

Another example of a successful businessperson who was too much in the Masculine Energy Vice of *disdain* was flamboyant hotelier Leona Helmsley. She was known for her tyrannical behavior and was ultimately dubbed the "Queen of Mean." Without empathy, she disdained and fired anyone on her staff who made the slightest mistake, shouting insults and obscenities as they were escorted out the door. Many of her employees turned out to cheer when she was locked up for tax evasion.

On the flipside are those who operate in the Feminine Energy Vice of *empathy* and are in danger of becoming *people-pleasers*, always worrying about how other people feel. They can become too empathetic, internalizing and imagining the feelings of others. In its extreme, they may even give feelings to inanimate objects, feeling sorry for wine glasses that aren't often used or chairs gathering dust in the attic.

Empathy is a valuable tool to cross the void and appreciate another's position, but it must be balanced with *rational* thinking, which confirms the old adage, "Educating the mind without educating the heart is no education at all."

Right Brain/Left Brain Virtues

Do you follow the recipe or creatively throw ingredients into the pan because you just know it will taste good?

Virtue Feminine	Vice Feminine	Virtue Masculine	Vice Masculine
Right brain	Overstimulation	Left brain	Compartmentalization

While conducting brain research at Harvard, neuroanatomist Jill Bolte Taylor suffered a massive stroke. Alone in her apartment, a blood vessel hemorrhaged on the left side of her brain and within four hours, she lost her ability to walk, talk, read, and write as well as her memories and her ability to think about the future. She later stated, however, that what came through from the right hemisphere of her brain was a deep feeling of inner peace. She could see the beauty of all things around her and felt an extensive sense of wonder and euphoria.

Because the left hemisphere was damaged and needed to be rebuilt following the stroke, she had lots of time to explore her right brain and came to understand its wisdom. In a best-selling book about her experience, entitled *My Stroke of Insight: A Brain Scientist's Personal Journey*, Bolte Taylor concludes that our culture prizes the admirable but often frantic work of the left brain, making us stressed, competitive, and often aggressive or argumentative. Both sides of the brain have their virtues, but she especially appreciates the value of the right brain.

Left-brain logic is enhanced by right-brain creativity

The benefits of Feminine Energy to the world became very evident in December 2015 at the climate change talks in Paris. World leaders came together to discuss runaway climate change, and it was the first time in history that 196 countries joined forces in a determined effort to save our planet. A critical mass of people from every sector imaginable set aside left-brain logic in searching for the creative solutions that are available only from the right brain.

Two participants at the Paris talks were Rachel Kyte, special envoy for climate change at the World Bank in the years leading up to the talks, and Nigel Topping, chief executive officer of the business coalition We Mean Business. Quoted in *HuffPost*, Kyte said that "the energy that emerged during the Paris talks was akin to the fierce love that a woman has when protecting her children." (Note how Feminine Energy love transforms into Masculine Energy to protect what is important.)

In the same article, Topping referred to this "'diplomacy of love' as having been critical to the success of the talks. I don't mean love in a kind of wishy-washy sense, but in a sense of real commitment to the whole, to the healing, to something bigger than the individual."

Clearly, Feminine Energy was essential to reaching an agreement, and it was delivered not only by the women at the table but also by the men who exercised these attributes. These participants, regardless of gender, looked beyond the Masculine Energy need to compete and utilized the capacity of collaboration to help save the planet.

The Masculine Energy *left-brain* Vice is *compartmentalization*, a defense mechanism used to avoid dealing with conflicting values, emotions, or beliefs. It is easier and more expedient to put things away in a mental box than to find a way to house dissenting views together. A strong argument could be made that the world was in this Vice before the Paris Agreement. Meanwhile, too much Feminine Energy (right brain) emphasis on the big picture results in the Vice of *overstimulation*: simple things become complex, the many connections create stumbling blocks, and people can't see the forest for the trees.

In Gender Physics terms, what Jill Bolte Taylor discovered and described is the overuse of Masculine Energy in our current world. It hurts not only our attempts to connect with others but also our ability to work together to create new ways of doing things. What she learned with her stroke, and also what the Paris climate change agreement taught us, is that when we access both sides of the brain using both Feminine and Masculine Energy, we not only live more fulfilling lives but can also institute great change.

Feeling/Thinking Virtues

Ever go shopping for some gardening tools and instead make an impulse decision to buy a brand-new outdoor grill?

Virtue Feminine	Vice Feminine	Virtue Masculine	Vice Masculine
Feeling	Overreacting	Thinking	Robotic

When it comes time to make a decision, it can be dangerous to use only *thinking* or only *feeling*. I learned this early in my career at PotashCorp. Market conditions were grim, with supply and demand dangerously out of balance, and our company results were in the red each month. In an attempt to revive the disheartened spirit of our salespeople, we brought them all together for a sales meeting.

As I was about to enter the dining hall the evening of the windup dinner, a personal mentor put his hand on my shoulder and asked for a minute of my time. While the boisterous voices of our sales team rang out from the room beyond, we spoke quietly in the hall. "Betty-Ann," he said gravely, "I know this isn't a pretty place to work right now, and it's only going to get worse. There are going to be a lot of changes, but I want you to hang on because this company needs people like you. It's a good company where you'll have a good career. I've worked in this business for thirty years, and I can tell you that it can turn on a dime. A mine can flood in Russia; China can come in with a big contract—supply and demand will suddenly rebalance, and we'll be back in the money." His parting words were, "Hang in."

Two weeks later, while on a business trip to the United States, I was standing in an airport pay-phone cubicle (these were the days before cell phones) when my secretary came on the line and told me to sit down. I silently obeyed and lowered myself onto the little triangular seat below, grimly waiting for her news. "Everybody on the floor above you has been fired," she said. The floor above me belonged to senior management, which meant the next proverbial bloodbath would likely take place in middle management. Morosely, I hung up the phone before continuing with my business, although my thoughts were understandably elsewhere during my customer visits that trip.

When I arrived back at the office, it was an ugly scene. Everyone knew that the first shoe had dropped and the other was still to come. It was an unpleasant period. Stress and backstabbing permeated the workplace; people strove to make others look bad to make themselves look good, all in a desperate attempt to retain their jobs.

When making a decision, it can be dangerous to use only *thinking* or only *feeling*

Eventually, it did happen—that is, the axe fell on the necks of many of my colleagues. Sadness and resentment filled the air, and I alleviated the burn by burying myself in my work. The more people who landed on the chopping block, the more work that landed on my plate. We had numerous commitments to our clients, yet half of the people responsible for keeping them were gone. I took on countless new responsibilities to help ensure that the company continued functioning the way it needed to. Even though I was busy and the days passed quickly, it was an incredibly difficult experience. People who were usually effective became incapable of making decisions, paralyzed with the fear of making a mistake and being fired. Budgets and salaries were frozen. I was working harder, putting in longer hours, and assuming extra responsibilities, without additional remuneration.

During all this, just when things seemed at their darkest, I received a lucrative job offer at another company. It was a very tempting opportunity. The job had a better title, a more public profile, and a well-established budget. My analytical *thinking* pointed to the exit, but when I imagined myself taking the job, there were real feelings of uncertainty niggling in my body. Even though it didn't logically make sense, I had a *feeling* that I should heed the advice of my now-fired mentor.

I remembered his reassurances: that the company was solid, that business could turn around quickly, and that I could establish an excellent career for myself if I just hung on. While this new opportunity was tempting, I decided to stick it out. The first day after making the decision, I felt happy and exuberant, convinced that it was right. The next day, when surrounded by the pessimism at the office, I was filled with doubt, wondering if I had been foolhardy and imprudent. But rather than allow these vacillating *feelings* to jerk me around like a yo-yo, I spent time *thinking* of the reasoning that got me there.

Too much thinking can result in us becoming robotic, like Spock

Of course my mentor was right—eventually, the world markets grew and came back into balance with supply. Soon thereafter, prices responded and we began to make money again. New management looked around and said, "Betty-Ann, you've picked up a lot of responsibility—it's time your title reflected that." And a salary increase soon followed.

Had I made my decision solely using rational *thinking*, I would have fallen into the Masculine Energy Vice of being *robotic*, like *Star Trek*'s Spock, famous for his absence of feelings. People who fall into this Vice overthink things, and because they are always seeking more information, they often have trouble making a decision. Feelings and emotion are the motivators behind taking action.

Conversely, if I had allowed my *feelings* to dial up out of control, I would have fallen into the Vice of being *overreactive*. I could have made my decision based on negative feelings such as fear, frustration, or disappointment and jumped ship without considering the golden opportunity where I was. Working with someone with this Vice isn't pleasant; they often use their feelings to manipulate others. There will always be someone in the office who, like Chicken Little, overreacts and claims the sky is falling. It is easy to tap into their sense of alarm, but a well-balanced leader will step in and provide a well-thought-out response.

Likewise, most offices will have someone who is so out of touch with their feelings that they are socially inept. These over-thinkers, in their effort to provide an honest assessment, can come across as critical. Again, a well-balanced leader will be conscious of how this affects feelings and will step in to provide a more tactful and conciliatory perspective.

For Feminine Energy *Heart* People to Develop Their Masculine Energy *Head*

Experiment with Facts If you lead with Feminine Energy in the *Heart/Head* Variable, you likely rely heavily on your feelings to decide what you think about something. You may exclaim with great disgust, "The restaurant was horrible," while someone with Masculine Energy would likely say, "The restaurant was overbooked and understaffed." Experiment with speaking only facts for one day each week. For example, instead of saying, "It's nice outside," say, "It's twenty-three degrees Celsius outside." Providing information accurately will not only give you confidence but also create valuable insights.

For Masculine Energy *Head* People to Develop Their Feminine Energy *Heart*

Experiment Supporting Others If you are a Masculine Energy person in the *Heart/Head* Variable, you are more likely to take an impersonal, objective approach to most things. You run the risk of treating others like problems to solve rather than people to relate to. Those with Feminine Energy connect with others and know the value of supporting the human who is having the problem. Experiment with letting go of the need to fix another's problems. Rather than automatically offering solutions, empathize and reflect back what others are feeling. This will show that you care.

Chapter Eight

Know/Go Variable

Knowing is not enough; we must apply.
Willing is not enough; we must do.
—*Johann Wolfgang von Goethe*

Characteristics of the Feminine Energy *Know* and the Masculine Energy *Go*

- In the *Know* Variable, Feminine Energy is content to observe the world and let it unfold.
- In the *Go* Variable, Masculine Energy is action oriented and wants to make things happen.

- In the *Know* Vices, those with Feminine Energy will become stagnant and repetitive.
- In the *Go* Vices, those with Masculine Energy will impetuously take action for the sake of action.

- When practicing Gender Physics and using both energies, people know they must rest and restore to get things done.

Typical Features of the Two Energies in This Variable

Feminine Energy: *Know*	Masculine Energy: *Go*
Gathers and holds information without action	Learns on the go
Believes where they are is where they are meant to be	Desires immediate change
Gives priority to the incubation and fertilization of ideas	Uses action as a measurement of progress
Sees the complexity of situations in shades of gray	Sees things simply, in black and white
Goes inside to learn about self	Learns about self through outside interactions
Derives knowledge from observation, like people-watching	Derives knowledge from participation
Sees big picture yet relishes small pleasures	Likes to focus on one course
Takes time to breathe and relax	Does and achieves in order to move forward

Know Is the Meditative Walk and *Go* Is the Mountain Climb

Think about two different journeys—one a slow meditative walk, the other a rigorous mountain climb. A meditative walk is taken at an easy pace. You might *reflect* while you're walking, *responding* to the subtlety and *nuance* of nature. You bask in the feel of the grass under your feet and the sun on your face. You do not worry about where you are walking because you simply follow the path; there is no need for caution or concern. You can *dream* and just *be*—that is the beauty of the Feminine Energy *Know* Variable.

The Masculine Energy *Go* Variable is climbing a mountain: you are in the *doing* mode, taking *action*. You have something to *achieve*, and it necessitates your full concentration to get there. When traversing a mountain, you must be focused and aware of every crevice and cranny as you *advance* toward the clear (and *simple*) objective: the task at hand. You cannot allow your mind to wander.

Know and Go Working Together Using Gender Physics

Queen Elizabeth I had a difficult childhood but grew up to become one of England's greatest monarchs, and she did it by demonstrating great balance between the Virtues of the *Know/ Go* Variable. Her history is well known: the execution of her mother, Anne Boleyn, by her father, King Henry Vlll; serial stepmothers as her father repeatedly (re)married; imprisonment in the Tower of London when her half-sister Mary I became queen … Yet as England's ruler, she expanded her country's trade, increased its wealth, defeated the Spanish Armada, and introduced legislation allowing theater to flourish.

Less well known is that when Elizabeth ascended the throne at age twenty-five, she had the knowingness to understand that she needed the support of the people to remain the queen, and she immediately began engendering their loyalty. During the country's lavish coronation celebrations, she stopped her procession on its way to Westminster to talk with ordinary citizens on the streets and reassure them that she had the power and conviction to be as good a queen as there ever was.

She had a vision of what she wanted to achieve and could see the complexity of the situation in shades of gray. This allowed her a pragmatic view of personal religion so she didn't rigorously enforce the rules of her Protestant church, further gaining the admiration of her people. Despite such leniency, she didn't hesitate to make black-and-white decisions and take action on them. She removed the pope as the head of the English church, chose not to marry despite pressure from her parliament, and financed Sir Walter Raleigh to circumnavigate the globe. In a wonderful early example of the benefits of using both energies, Queen Elizabeth I is quoted as saying: "I know I have the body of a weak and feeble woman, but I have the heart and stomach of a king, and a king of England too." This is probably as close as you can get to Gender Physics in the sixteenth century!

Getting to Know the Virtues, and Their Vices

In the *Know/Go* Variable, there is an overarching desire of Feminine Energy people to let the world unfold as it will while those who prefer Masculine Energy want to be on the go. Each can be expressed by five related Virtues, which are strengths when used in appropriate amounts but, when used in absolute terms, can morph into Vices, or weaknesses.

Know Virtue (Feminine Energy Strengths)	*Go* Virtue (Masculine Energy Strengths)
Reflection	Action
Dream	Achieve
Being	Doing
Respond	Advance
Nuance	Simplification

***Know* Virtues** (Feminine Energy Strengths)	***Know* Vices** (Feminine Energy Weaknesses)
Reflection	Perfectionism
Dream	Fool's paradise
Being	Disengaged
Respond	Paralysis
Nuance	Irrelevancy

***Go* Virtues** (Masculine Energy Strengths)	***Go* Vices** (Masculine Energy Weaknesses)
Action	Recklessness
Achieve	Overambitious
Doing	Compulsive
Advance	Overreaching
Simplification	Distortion

Analyzing YOU

In Appendix 2, the Go-To Energy Evaluation, total your scores separately in each part for questions 26 to 30 (inclusive). If your score is higher in part 1, you operate from Feminine Energy *Know* in this Variable. If your score is higher in part 2, your behavior is Masculine Energy *Go* in this Variable.

Reflection/Action Virtues

Do you really like this person enough to get their name tattooed on your bicep?

Virtue Feminine	Vice Feminine	Virtue Masculine	Vice Masculine
Reflection	Perfectionism	Action	Recklessness

While at the Columbia Business School in New York, I partici-pated in a team-building exercise that provided a lesson on the value of balancing both the Masculine Energy of *action* with the Feminine Energy of *reflection*. My group, a mix of twelve men and women, stood blindfolded in a field, holding hands as we listened carefully to our instructor describe our task. We were a little nervous and anxious to succeed not only because we wanted to impress our classmates, who were corporate executives from leading global companies, but also because the exercise was being videotaped to show future classes.

The task itself seemed straightforward enough. At our feet lay two lengths of rope. We were expected to make a square out of the long piece of rope. Then, inside the square, we were to make a triangle out of the short piece of rope. There were only two rules: we had twenty minutes to complete the challenge; and once we touched the rope, we could move along the rope but were not allowed to let go. With these parameters, the simple task became a little more complex.

The moment the whistle blew, most of the men and one Masculine Energy woman from our group immediately hunched down to pick up the rope. "All right, let's get going," they chimed in chorus. Most of the women and one Feminine

Energy man continued to tightly hold hands to prevent them from touching the ropes.

"Hold it! Hold it! Hold it! Let's *reflect* on this a moment," said one of the Feminine Energy group members who was clearly quite capable of using Masculine Energy to make their voice heard.

With that, everyone took a deep breath and calmed down. Then talking quickly, everyone threw out ideas to solve the problem. Skilled at measuring fabric from my sewing days, I offered to measure the ropes and once that was determined, I could divide the longer rope into quarters and tie three knots to mark off the quarters.

"I'll take the first corner," volunteered one person.

"Right, then I'll take the second one," volunteered another. With that we were off to the races, building on one another's suggestions.

The Feminine Energy people in our group were determined to hold hands and talk through the plan until every last detail was ironed out, which, given our time limitations, was not the best idea. Luckily, there were also action-oriented Masculine Energy people in our group who prodded us into taking more decisive *action*: "We have a good plan, but we're running out of time here!" they pleaded. "We need to get going … if we don't hurry up, we'll miss our deadline, and all this good planning will be for naught." Taking a deep breath and focusing our concentration, we dropped our hands and executed our plan.

Those with Masculine Energy are unlikely to miss a deadline

At the twenty-minute mark, we pulled off our blindfolds. What a sight we must have made: twelve business executives, jumping up and down with glee to see a perfect triangle inside a perfect square. Our instructor was thoroughly impressed and, in congratulating us, said that she had never seen such a good result. We basked in our collective glory as we found seats on the sidelines.

Now it was our turn to watch another group—this one all male—perform the same exercise. As soon as the start whistle blew, they snatched up the ropes and set to work, attempting to concoct a strategy as they went along. Of course, they all grabbed the ropes, so none of them could let go. They decided two members of their group, Jim and Tom, would each walk with a rope to determine which was longer, but of course they were blindfolded so they couldn't see. Several of them tripped.

"Who sounds the farthest away?"

"Jim ... I think!"

"No, it's Tom."

"Who?"

"What?"

It was a disaster, and ultimately, they gave up even before reaching the time limit. We laughed to the point of tears as the entangled men attempted to sort themselves out. "You need a woman in there to keep you from getting ahead of yourselves!" one of the executives in the audience shouted.

One of the blindfolded and flustered men was an executive for a huge automobile manufacturer that was close to bankruptcy. "No wonder your company is in so much trouble," we teased him afterward. "You're just jumping in and making cars without any planning or reflection."

People in organizations often have tug-of-wars when those with Feminine Energy seek to reflect while those with Masculine

Energy want immediate action. Obviously, the Masculine Energy Virtue of taking *action* is valuable (as it was for our group). However, if it is dialed up to the extreme, it can fall into the Vice of *recklessness*, where someone acts in haste with complete lack of concern for the consequences of their actions. We saw this in the all-male group that, upon hearing the whistle, recklessly reached for the ropes. They could have made it work if some of those men had shifted into their Feminine Energy and assumed the role of *reflection*. Instead, they succumbed to Gender Pull, as often happens when a group consisting of only one gender is assembled. That gender conditioning from an early age is hard to kick. In this case, it was men with Masculine Energy seeking action.

Conversely, if our group had stayed only in its Feminine Energy, we could have gone on planning and reflecting for-*evah*! In fact, succumbing to the Vice of *perfectionism*, we'd probably still be there trying to make our plan flawless. We'd have missed our deadline, and nothing would ever have been accomplished.

> **Those with Feminine Energy can reflect too much and too long looking for perfection**

I have been prone to fall into this Vice. On my desk sits a glass paperweight with an important question carved into one side: "What would you do if you had no fear?" One day, a friend who was visiting my office asked me how I would answer the question. Without hesitation, I said, "Give up perfectionism."

Perfectionism comes from the fear that our strengths and abilities are not enough, that they will not stand on their own. Overcompensating by trying to be perfect drains not only our time and energy but also the fun from our experiences. It can also limit our dreams because we pass up opportunities due to the fear that we might not be … perfect. The fear that our achievements aren't enough has us spending too long editing the perfect report, overplanning the perfect event, or holding back in a meeting to formulate the perfect comment.

Falling into the Vice of perfectionism erodes self-confidence, which ironically increases fear and results in the demand for even more perfectionism. In his book *What Happy People Know: How the New Science of Happiness Can Change Your Life for the Better,* Dan Baker describes perfectionism as a demon pretending to be a strength. We improperly credit perfectionism, not our abilities and competence, for our achievements. "Fear doesn't emerge as nail-biting, cold-feet terror but surfaces instead as perfectionism," he says.

It is important to *reflect* before moving forward, but you can't wait until you have the perfect plan; often you'll have to take *action* before you feel ready. Likewise, if you don't take the time to reflect before you jump in, you will inevitably end up haplessly wiping grass stains from your knees!

Dream/Achieve Virtues

The best part of looking at photos of others' travels is that you can imagine where you want to go!

Virtue Feminine	Vice Feminine	Virtue Masculine	Vice Masculine
Dream	Fool's paradise	Achieve	Overambitious

In my role as a senior VP, I mentored several emerging leaders. I remember once dropping by the office of a promising young woman who worked in IT to ask why she hadn't applied for an opening that was being offered in my department. She told me that it was her dream to work in the head office, but she was unsure about her ability to assume the responsibilities that were needed in this new and unfamiliar position. Also, she knew that my department had a lot of interaction with the CEO, and she was afraid of being put under pressure and in the spotlight while she was learning on the job.

I explained to her that one of the benefits of being on the radar screen of senior management is that there is more chance for vertical promotions, and I reassured her that she was ready and more than capable. She needed to start experimenting with her career. Having a *dream* is great, but if you don't have a method to *achieve* it, you'll never make any progress. It was time for this young woman to shift from the Feminine Energy attribute of *dreaming* and start using her Masculine Energy to *achieve*. And while we were on the topic of dreaming, I suggested that she go home, sleep on it, and come back to see me the next day.

Sitting in my office the next morning, she solemnly said that she had decided not to apply. I raised my eyebrows since her answer didn't ring true. She went on to tell me that she knew she would really like the position, but her head told her she was comfortable where she was. That's when I told her that to *achieve*, she needed to take a risk. She needed to follow her heart and take action to fulfill her *dream*. I was reluctant to push too hard as the decision had to be hers, yet I hated to see her immobilized due to an overabundance of caution. It took a bit more convincing, but ultimately, she applied for the job, won it, and has never looked back. That was the first of many promotions, and it has been very gratifying to watch her career progress.

Dreaming and *achieving* used together successfully has provided the world with many important and beneficial discoveries.

Canadian scientist Julia Levy had a dream to help her mother, who suffered from macular degeneration. She hated her mother's discomfort and wanted to help rescue her from the debilitating disease. Using her skills and talents, she designed a light-activated drug that has since become a breakthrough treatment for more than two million people in more than eighty countries worldwide. In fact, her invention—photodynamic therapy—was the germination of a high-achieving biotechnology company called QLT Inc.

Those with Feminine Energy are motivated to improve the lives of others, which spurs innovation

Like Julia Levy, countless inventors are motivated by their Feminine Energy to improve the lives of others. There are also those who, driven by their Masculine Energy, want to make their individual mark on things. Neither motivation is wrong, as both are simply starting points. An idea doesn't come to fruition without confidence, and an invention that doesn't consider the end user will never make it to market. We need the balance of both.

Certainly, we must guard against leaning too far into the Feminine Energy Virtue of *dreaming*, which can have us entering the Vice of a *fool's paradise,* a state of delusion based on false beliefs. In the grasp of this Vice, we can easily remain completely unrealistic, dismissing contradictory evidence. We've probably all worked with someone who really is in a suspended-animation state on some issue and we just want them to wake up. By having a dream yet thinking she could achieve it without taking action, the young woman at my company had entered that territory. Her fear of failure kept her from trying things, which squandered her dream and limited her achievements.

Fortunately, she did wake up and take the risk, and the story has a happy ending.

Equally as ineffective as living in a dream world is leaning too hard into Masculine Energy—wanting *achievement* so desperately that we become *overambitious*. In this Vice, we relentlessly and incessantly pursue more accomplishments, many of them meaningless. Those who are *overambitious* are never satisfied. Once they accomplish a desired outcome, they turn their attention to the next project. It is akin to being a hamster on a wheel. In perpetual action, they don't allow themselves the time to dream of what could be, and perhaps many good inventions never come to be.

To move from the Feminine Energy safety of *dreaming* about our goals into the Masculine Energy action of *achieving* them, we need balance and we need courage. Courage, much like confidence, develops from doing, experimenting, and then trying again. We get more by doing more.

Being/Doing Virtues

When on a hike, do you enjoy nature or immediately catalog the flora and fauna?

Virtue Feminine	Vice Feminine	Virtue Masculine	Vice Masculine
Being	Disengaged	Doing	Compulsive

When we are young, we feel we can do anything, that the possibilities are endless. Ballet or soccer, math or art, downhill skiing or gymnastics ... all are possibilities and among the things that we can choose to do. As we move through life, however, we find that the choices open to us are fewer, and as they diminish, we realize that there are only so many things that we can mentally or physically accomplish. It took a diagnosis in my mid-thirties for me to realize that I needed more Feminine Energy in my life. I desperately needed more *being* and less *doing*.

As the primary breadwinner for my family, I worked full-time and had two baby girls close in age. With each child, I continued working until the day before I gave birth and returned to work six weeks later. Along with my male colleagues, I ignored that I was a new mother, and it was not unusual for one of them to stop by my office at noon to request that I be on a plane by 5 P.M. I was trying to be one of them as well as a good mother, so I continued to nurse my babies and express milk on the road. Needless to say, I became exhausted.

Not surprisingly, I eventually became ill, and my doctor informed me that I had mononucleosis. She predicted a recovery period that would range from three weeks to three months. But after three months, fatigue continued to pummel me. I returned to the doctor multiple times, but the lab tests revealed little. Although I didn't know it at the time, I had another two years of symptoms ahead of me. I felt physically depleted. My friends suggested exercise, but a walk around the block left me more exhausted than refreshed. I still remember the daily discomfort of living with every gland in my body being constantly tender and painfully swollen.

I continued to work during this period, but concluded each day by collapsing on the couch. Accepting social engagements was out of the question. My weakened immune system left me vulnerable to any bug that was circulating in the office, and if I caught something, I would revert to the initial acute stages of mono in which I slept for days on end. Crawling out of bed for a glass of orange juice so debilitated me that I was soon back in bed, sleeping again.

Throughout the next couple of years, visiting my doctor in hopes of a diagnosis became a constant part of my routine. She would send me to the lab with every box method- ically ticked off—but invariably, every test would come back negative. It was extremely disheartening. I knew I was sick, yet my tests continually, maddeningly declared me healthy. I remember my doctor telling me, "If you were a different kind of person, I would suggest that you were suffering from depression, but I just don't believe that's the case."

By doing too much, my Masculine Energy was out of balance

It was interesting to hear this, because it felt the other way around. I was getting depressed from being sick. Every time I looked at a happy radiant person on a magazine cover, I would feel angry at the injustice in the world. They were healthy and enjoying life while I was ailing and dragging myself around. I would mentally challenge them to appreciate their good luck and then fall further into a funk.

Finally, my doctor sent me for evaluation to the Infectious Diseases division in the University of Saskatchewan Department of Medicine. After a series of tests and examinations, the doctors gave me an official diagnosis of Epstein-Barr virus. I was the first person in Saskatchewan to be diagnosed with the illness, a precursor to chronic fatigue syndrome. Epstein-Barr virus was first chronicled in medical journals in January 1983; I received my diagnosis in May of the same year. This was a good news/ bad news story. My illness had been identified, so that was good news, but the virus was still too new for doctors to suggest a treatment. I decided that if there was nothing medical science could do for me, there must be something I could do for myself. This was prior to the Internet, so I went to the library and checked out books about people who had overcome chronic and terminal diseases, hoping to find a common thread in their stories.

As it turns out, the common thread was using meditation and visualizing oneself healthy. Meditation increases alpha brain waves, which, incidentally, promotes self-healing. I had some university friends who had taken up Transcendental Meditation (TM) and enthused about their results, but the lessons cost $500—$500 that I didn't have. So I made another trip to the library, to borrow all the books I could find on meditation. In 1985 in Saskatoon, this quest resulted in a grand total of five small books. Still, I was determined and managed to teach myself how to meditate. I had almost immediate results. After a few weeks, I was able to accept social engagements, and after a few short months, if someone in the office had a flu or cold, I didn't catch it!

What I needed was time to just be in my Feminine Energy

By trying to be a good mother, spouse, and full-time executive, while striving to further my career, I was exerting too much Masculine Energy. I was consumed with *doing*. Viruses are around us all the time, and they are opportunistic. When you become rundown by doing too much, you create an opportunity for a virus to pass by your natural immunity. Recovery from an illness requires that we slow down and rest so our body can heal itself.

What I truly needed was the time to simply *be*, to center myself so that I could slip into a quiet state of self-reflection. Those who do this to the extreme fall into the Vice of being *disengaged*. They enter their own little world and stop being involved with others. I was never in danger of this total release of attachment since I was full-blown in the opposite direction, consumed by the Masculine Energy Vice of *compulsiveness*.

By doing too much, I was completely out of balance to the detriment of my health and well-being. If you had looked in the dictionary under "compulsive workaholic," you could have found my picture. Meditation turned out to be the missing factor I needed to be able to oscillate successfully between the two energies. My personal struggle with balancing Masculine and Feminine Energies demonstrates that what we teach is sometimes what we most need to learn.

Respond/Advance Virtues

Do you help your friends with assignments before doing your own?

Virtue Feminine	Vice Feminine	Virtue Masculine	Vice Masculine
Respond	Paralysis	Advance	Overreaching

I'm always impressed by the caliber of films presented at TIFF, and 2016 was no exception. During the first week of the festival, we viewed the premiere of *Below Her Mouth*, a passionate love story between two women. During the Q and A that followed the screening, the female director remarked that the love scenes would have been very different had a male directed them. In reaction, a man sitting close to the front of the theater was quick to jump up and ask her to clarify the comment. She answered that, characteristically, of paramount importance to a male director would have been the sexual act itself, and the relationship would be framed from that viewpoint (read *advance* the sexual consummation as opposed to *respond* to your partner). Seen through the eyes of a female director, the relationship became about the intimacy between the women, so the focus was on the emotions felt and the looks that passed between the lovers rather than simply accelerating to a climax.

Allowing others to *respond* and measuring actions based on that is Feminine Energy, while *advancing* the story, strategy, or game is Masculine Energy. As the example demonstrates, the preponderance of male directors act out their Gender Pull and are focused on advancing the story.

Taken to the extreme, this marching forward can become a Vice, where one *overreaches* attempting to gain too much and misses the mark. People in this Vice often don't accept limitations, get in over their heads, and tend to push too far. When companies try to advance their objectives without stopping to check if they are acting in response to market sentiment, they are likely to face roadblocks and see sporadic, haphazard results.

> Gender Pull can be avoided when individuals become more aware

Responding to the needs of employees, customers, or investors is a Feminine Energy Virtue. However, when taken to a hyper-response, it can breed the Vice of *paralysis*. You've probably witnessed people at work who have a disgruntled client, but afraid of conflict, they avoid calling them altogether. Rather than getting to the bottom of the issue and offering consistent, responsive service, they ignore the problem and eventually lose the client.

A good example of using Gender Physics to *advance* a successful film by taking into account the expected *response* of the audience was 2017's *All the Money in the World*. The film was finished, with Kevin Spacey playing the lead role of J. Paul Getty, but when the actor was accused of sexual abuse, the director made an unprecedented decision and replaced him with Christopher Plummer. That meant reshooting twenty-two scenes over nine days, and included working over American Thanksgiving, but they got it done.

When it comes to filmmaking, in 2017, nearly 90 percent of directors were male, but some are in tune with their Feminine Energy and, when behind the camera, shoot scenes in a very emotional and nurturing way. With this sensitive approach, established stereotypes just naturally fall away. We view the world through a lens that is certainly influenced by our conditioning but need not necessarily be determined by our sex. Gender Pull can be avoided when individuals become more aware, which will, in turn, make space for all kinds of stories to be told in all kinds of ways.

Nuance/Simplification Virtues

Why do you attest that you don't like fish, yet you eat it deep-fried?

Virtue Feminine	Vice Feminine	Virtue Masculine	Vice Masculine
Nuance	Irrelevancy	Simplification	Distortion

You may know that many snakes bear certain patterns and colors that indicate whether or not they are poisonous. In order to determine whether you're facing a nonpoisonous kingsnake or a deadly coral snake, one can use the following mnemonic: "Red next to black is a friend of Jack. Red next to yellow can kill a fellow." You could spend time inspecting snakes for such nuances, but given the risk, most of us want certainty and simply avoid all snakes.

Iain McGilchrist penned a book called *The Master and His Emissary: The Divided Brain and the Making of the Western World*. In it, he describes a general standing before a control room map. The general says, "Tomorrow we are going into battle. We'll advance from A to B to C to D." He is certain about his plan and has *simplified* the big picture—but he needs to be careful not to forget the *nuances*. The general needs to know that between A and B is a forest, and between B and C is a swamp. Considering these nuances and how to address them in his plan can make the difference between a successful and an unsuccessful mission. The *simplification* is the context, and the *nuance* is the subtlety and sophistication. Of course, when giving the *nuance*, it is important not to get bogged down in *irrelevant* detail such as how to fight at sea when going over land.

Nuance is what you read between the lines, and it's a Feminine Energy attribute

In every business, there are *nuances*, things that aren't quite as simple as they might seem, and often only insiders are aware of them. Our business was no different, and the following scene was not unusual.

The portfolio manager across the table took a long drink of water, rolled up his sleeves, and carefully eyed up our CEO—perhaps looking for even a bead of perspiration where his brightly colored tie with its perfect Windsor knot met his crisp white shirt. But in the warm, stale air of the conference room, he found none. Then with just a hint of attitude, the portfolio manager challenged him: "If you truly are the lowest-cost producer, why don't you run your plants full out and put everybody out of business?"

Through slightly narrowed eyes, my CEO stared at the portfolio manager, as though at an insolent schoolboy. "I know that sounds simple, but it doesn't reflect the intricacies of this business," he said slowly, stopping short of adding "sonny"—but just barely. "And I have watched as many producers tried that tack and nearly ran themselves out of business in the process. It never works."

He always enjoyed being the expert with control of the floor, and I could see him relax slightly in his chair as he readied to step into the benevolent father role (one he relished). Becoming very patient, his voice softened and he adopted the demeanor of a storyteller. "The potash business has high barriers obstructing entry, and putting in a mine is a *very* expensive proposition," he explained. "Once the initial investment has been made, people do not just 'walk away'; they run their plants for cash costs. No— our competitors will keep on producing, and there is nothing we can do to stop that. We simply have to wait until growing world demand allows us to use our excess capacity."

He then went on to reminisce about how he had learned this lesson early in his career when running a potash plant. He had pushed his guys hard to reduce production costs, and his team was euphoric when they managed to accomplish a reduction of five dollars a ton. However, when they went to their monthly management meeting expecting to be congratulated for their contribution to the bottom line, they were disappointed to discover that the company was no further ahead. Because of the tough market, the sales guys had lowered their prices by five dollars a ton. In fact, they came to the meeting and announced with excitement, "We maintained our market share." It was then that my CEO realized that focusing on market share was not the answer. He decided that if ever he was given the opportunity to run a company, he would focus on the price and make sure every ton he sold would be at a profit.

Then my boss seemingly turned the tables. For him, meetings were as tactical as his market-driven sales strategy. He was not going to backpedal or withdraw, *and* he threw out a reverse challenge to the portfolio manager.

"If you must have earnings this quarter, we're not the stock for you. You should sell your investment in us."

The portfolio manager didn't hesitate. "No. I'm happy with your answers," he said, and smiled with satisfaction. They shook hands and we exited the meeting.

Too much emphasis on nuance can result in irrelevant detail

The portfolio manager's position was typical of investors, and we would often have to explain the *nuances* of the industry. You might think that our CEO would get bored with the re-explaining, but you would be wrong. Because he operated with so much Masculine Energy, being challenged brought him to life. He would straighten his back, lean forward, and punctuate his words to make his point. "Let me tell you why price undercutting would never work."

Sometimes we have a miscommunication with someone and our meaning is misconstrued. It could be that our body language or tone of voice sends a different message than our words. This *nuance* was explained in a short but unforgettable scene in the film *Donnie Brasco*. Playing the part of an undercover agent who infiltrates a crime family, Johnny Depp explains how *fugetaboutit* can mean entirely different things depending on intonation. It could mean, "the sex was great, the car is bad, or quit teasing me about the size of my ..." Only the insiders know the secret language to get it right.

Simplification has been widely touted as a competitive advantage in business, as it allows us to maintain clarity and avoids getting bogged down in unnecessary complexity. There is so much noise in the marketplace that we need simple, crystallized messages. However, when we oversimplify a subject and don't include enough detail, it can become a Vice that misleads. By moving too far into simplification, a kind of *distortion* occurs where, like a funhouse mirror, nothing is as it appears and reality isn't reflected clearly. In a world prone to information overload, we are constantly being told to skip unnecessary details, but this type of omission can result in errors. As Albert Einstein said, "Everything should be made as simple as possible, but not simpler."

Masculine Energy is good at not getting weighed down in unnecessary detail and complexity

On the other side, if we lean too far into *nuance*, we will find the Vice of *irrelevancy*, where we are so hung up in the details that we'll find ourselves examining lots of things that are not even pertinent. We'll end up first confusing and then losing our audience.

Finding the balance Einstein recommends comes from injecting the Virtue with its Complement before it becomes a Vice. *Simplification* gives meaning to the *nuance* while *nuance* provides substance for *simplification*.

For Feminine Energy *Know* People to Develop Their Masculine Energy *Go*

Experiment with Taking Risks If you lead with Feminine Energy in the *Know/Go* Variable, you'll be prone to perfectionism and damaging bouts of self-criticism if you make mistakes. For example: "One of the calculations was wrong in the spreadsheet; therefore, I am a bad person." This faulty thinking can lead to paralysis and immobility. Experiment with taking action by starting with small, calculated risks. It's better to try meditating for five minutes than to take five courses on meditation in an effort to do it perfectly. Get ready to learn by doing. Accept that not every risk will deliver the results you desire, that you will make some small mistakes, and that you may not always get the praise you crave. But one thing is certain: the biggest risk is to hold back and not do anything. Find something you feel strongly about and take even a baby-step action. Confidence comes from taking action. As the Nike slogan says, "Just Do It."

For Masculine Energy *Go* People to Develop Their Feminine Energy *Know*

Experiment with Spontaneity If your Go-To Energy is Masculine in the *Know/Go* Variable, it is important for you to feel productive and you are apt to be all work and no play. Those with Feminine Energy create authentic, spontaneous experiences that may have no other purpose than simply pleasure. Experiment with being more emergent, flexible, and adaptable. Let go of your need to be doing something all the time. Take time for nonproductive things like paging through a coffee table book or calling someone just to say "Hi" when you think of them. And remember to mobilize your senses. Those with Feminine Energy don't just look—they see things as if they are looking at them for the first or last time. They notice the chirping of the birds and the aroma of coffee, and they take time to savor their food. Experiment with pausing and taking a deep breath to truly connect with the world.

Chapter Nine

So What?
Now What?

There is no such thing as work-life balance—
it is all life. The balance has to be within you.

—*Sadhguru*

We have now learned that each of us has a Go-To Energy that could be different from our biological gender and that we are made up of myriad attributes, preferring Masculine Virtues in some Variables and Feminine in others. That results in each of us being a unique and individual energy combination. Practicing Gender Physics allows both energies to emerge and work together so we can balance them, since an overabundance of either energy is problematic. Yet, to do that, we must overcome our Gender Pull and stop responding to situations by doing what is expected of us simply because that is how it has always been done.

Progress does not come from repeatedly doing the same thing, but new ideas are not always welcomed with open arms (at least not until the new idea succeeds) because people are resistant to change. Throughout history, many pioneers and explorers were shunned—sometimes even considered mad—for having advanced innovations. Had they listened to the masses and stood still, they would never have made new discoveries or improved on old concepts.

They were motivated to expand their horizons and make change because they no longer believed in the old way of doing things and wanted better. I hope that you do, too, and are now convinced it is worth taking advantage of both Masculine and Feminine Energies. That will provide you with the necessary commitment and conviction to move forward.

This chapter gives you the tools to step outside your comfort zone and make balancing the energies a reality in your life. We discuss how to attempt the unfamiliar and use the revolutionary Gender Physics framework to change the way we interact in the world. We introduce a behavioral change model to experiment with, and we refer to the Variables, Virtues, and Vices discussed in the preceding six chapters. I know there are a lot of words! Please don't try to commit them to memory. Instead, use the list in Appendix 3 as a reference.

Giving Purposeful Thought to Change

Learning how to ride a bike took concentration, trial and error, and failure before finally meeting with success. First, you needed to experiment until you found the right balance and it became second nature. The same is true of learning the Gender Physics balance. To change successfully, we need to give purposeful thought to changing. We need to reflect and then practice, until ultimately, we have established a new way of doing something. This is living with intention.

Even with awareness, most people do not like the experience of change, because it is uncomfortable. Try this (not so) simple exercise to appreciate how awkward change feels. Take a piece of paper and sign your name. Easy, right? Likely, it is something that you do without even thinking about it. Now take the pen in your other hand and sign your name again. How did that feel? Odd, right? It's possible, but it feels very strange, and if given the choice, you would always choose to use your dominant hand. However, if you continued to practice writing with your other hand, with time and some effort, you would eventually get better at it.

Later on, if someone were to ask you to sign something, your automatic reflex would still be to use your dominant hand (unless you stopped for a moment and chose to use your other hand). It takes mindful will and exercising choice to make any change that is significant. Even after you have made the change, it is very easy to go back to the way you were before the change. Your Go-To Energy is the same: you show up using a certain energy because of your unconscious bias for that energy. True growth occurs when you are aware of your dominant Go-To Energy preference but choose to use the other energy ... your Complementary Energy.

Unlike handwriting, your Go-To Energy may not always be the right choice. Suppose that Feminine Energy is your natural inclination, and that means you are usually observant and a good listener. However, it also means you are reticent about offering your views during management meetings. But when alone with your thoughts after the meetings, invariably, you feel frustrated that the management team makes decisions without asking your opinion. In fact, sometimes the consensus they reach is totally the opposite of what you believe is the best solution. To realize a different outcome, you must try a different approach. Take the handwriting exercise one step further to open yourself to behavior changes. It can help you find your voice so that your opinions can be heard in the management meeting.

Start by writing the following question with your dominant hand: "How do I become more assertive in management meetings?" Use your nondominant hand to write this answer: "I will listen and consider others' opinions, but when I have something to say, I am going to speak up. I am going to lay out my concerns and my solutions. I am going to speak clearly and with authority when stating my point."

In the same way that the experience of writing the answer with your nondominant hand is not easy or comfortable (or even legible), being more assertive may not be easy or comfortable for you either. But you tried what was uncomfortable for you, and … you wrote your name. You did it! You embedded an idea in your brain in a new way. If you try it again tomorrow, it will be a little easier, and the day after, easier still. It is the same in learning to shift energies.

To realize a different outcome, you must try a different approach

Consider when your next meeting comes up: although you may not feel completely at ease about it, you know what you must do and how you must act if you want to be more assertive and be heard. Then, when you act in those ways and find the courage to speak up, you will have circumvented your unconscious bias. During the meeting, you could even try taking some notes with your nondominant hand about points that you want to make when you have the attendees' attention (or maybe not—you might need to be able to read them).

Experiment with Gender Physics in the Workplace

The workplace has many different people with different energy combinations. Some of us might be highly independent and, therefore, Masculine Energy in the *We/Me* Variable, yet very laid-back and Feminine Energy in the *Know/Go* Variable. With our countless energy combinations, working with or managing people who hold opposite opinions can feel a little like a tug-of-war. It's not unusual for those goal-oriented Masculine Energy people to be impatient with those Feminine Energy people who want to spend more time on the process. Another source of friction often comes when those with Masculine Energy are totally focused on the bottom line while Feminine Energy managers are vigilant about how company actions will affect stakeholders.

To find common ground and see the value in the other, we have to change our point of reference. If it is our employees who are polarized, it helps to challenge their conflicting opinions. Laura Yecies, while CEO of SugarSync, provided some good guidance on how to do this in an interview in the July 9, 2012, *New York Times*. Yecies said that employees would come to her and say, "So-and-so is really giving me a hard time. They're not doing XYZ. I'm really mad." She describes how these employees go on and on about how bad the other person is and compares it to the sibling rivalry that you hear from kids. Yecies recommends disarming them by saying, "So they're doing this thing that you don't like. Do you think they're doing it because they think that's the better way to get the job done, or do you think that they're acting that way because they don't want us to be successful?" Of course, the person complaining must acknowledge that their coworker isn't acting as they are to sabotage the company. Furthermore, they have to admit that their coworker *also* thinks that they are going about things in the best possible way. People forget that everyone is trying to do the right thing and that the disagreement comes from tactics or strategy, Yecies explained.

When faced with these situations, I also found that sending the complaining employee off to gather information on why their peer thought there was a better way of doing things broke down resistance and healed misunderstandings. Most often they recognized a different side of the argument, and occasionally, the two adversaries came up with a previously unexplored alternative that was superior to what either of them had advocated previously.

Use Gender Physics to find common ground by changing your frame of reference

This technique of finding common ground can be used with our employees, and we can use it on ourselves. The next time someone disagrees with you at work, remember that you both want the same thing: the success of the company.

Before arguing, realize that you are approaching the situation from your frame of reference and with your Go-To Energy. Take the time to mentally approach it from their frame of reference and their Go-To Energy. For example, you might be concerned about the long-term ramifications of an action while they are citing the short-term benefits. Take their position and mentally go through all their reasoning. Then when you enter the discussion, you'll be able to talk about the advantages of their position as well as your own. By using this simple practice, you'll have a chance to use the Gender Physics platform of *both* energies by addressing the long-term concerns while still taking advantage of the short-term opportunities.

In his book *Polarity Management,* author Barry Johnson describes how looking at the whole picture can help you manage paradoxical relationships more effectively by expanding your own reality. "It is easier to expand your view than to get your opposition to expand theirs," he says. And "once you have seen the accuracy of the other person's view, it becomes relatively easy to shift back and forth between the two perceptions." Additionally, holding your position while integrating its opposite is what management guru Jim Collins describes in his book *From Good to Great: Why Some Companies Make the Leap ... And Others Don't.* He says that a visionary company doesn't want to blend yin and yang into a gray indistinguishable circle that is neither highly yin nor highly yang; it aims to be distinctly yin (Feminine Energy) and distinctly yang (Masculine Energy)— both at the same time, all the time.

Learning to keep your energy from dialing up to the extreme, escaping your Gender Pull, and holding your position while integrating its opposite takes experimentation. It is an opportunity to apply the learning. Next, we provide some ideas of things you can try.

Experiments for Developing Your Complementary Energy

- Feminine Energy people can develop their Masculine Energy by observing and spending time with groups of men. Due to socialization and gender conditioning, approximately 70 percent of men will have a Go-To Energy that is Masculine, and when they come together in groups, they exhibit these characteristics even more strongly. (Remember that we are all chameleons, so we pick up the characteristics of those with whom we spend time.) Feminine Energy people give compliments as an equalizer, while those with Masculine Energy play one-upmanship by giving one another shots to establish a hierarchy. He who gives the best shot wins! A new young female engineer learned this on her first day underground. Naturally nervous and wanting to be accepted, she was thrown off when one of the guys looked at her, raised his eyebrows, and said, "Nice socks." She then spent the remainder of her day worrying about her socks. Should they have been folded? Tucked in her pants? Eventually, she figured out that this shot about her socks meant she was being included. If she wanted to move up the hierarchy, she had to play the game and send out some put-downs as well. It was such a different way of showing acceptance. So for Feminine Energy people, experiment by entering the Masculine Energy game—take a tiny, playful shot and have some fun with it!

- Masculine Energy people can develop their Feminine Energy by observing and spending time with groups of women, because again, due to Gender Pull approximately 70 percent of women have Go-To Feminine Energy. Our brains develop based on what we see around us, so those with Masculine energy can develop their Complementary Energy by taking liberal arts classes, reading books written by women, and spending time in predominantly female-centric organizations such as preschool parenting cooperatives. To level the playing field, Feminine Energy people make a ritual of praising others, and it's common to hear women who meet one another for the first time say, "I like your shoes ... Good haircut! ... etc. These words of recognition go a long way. As Mark Twain once said, "I can live for two months on a good compliment." Experiment with offering compliments on someone's sense of humor, ability to bring a meeting to consensus, dedication to the team, or talent for finding creative solutions. (In work situations, males should avoid giving females compliments on appearance as they can be misconstrued.) Also, organizations tend to undervalue behind-the-scenes work most often done by women, such as avoiding a crisis or building a team. Instead, companies reward courageous risk-taking most often done by men. Thus, Masculine Energy leaders should openly thank those with Feminine Energy for their collaborative skills and for being risk aware. They will feel included and appreciated, and it will encourage them to provide the balanced opinion that can help companies avoid stepping in some serious sinkholes.

- There are many Feminine Energy attributes such as compassion, collaboration, and bringing people to a consensus, but they all boil down to showing others that you care. Ask how someone is doing and then ... really listen to the answers. In group situations, rather than passing over less vocal coworkers to reach a resolution or decision, try to draw out their thoughts. The increased time spent conceptualizing is likely to pay long-term dividends because of the wider range of ideas that will be available to you. Additionally, these Feminine Energy actions will engender loyalties and build up trust.

- To increase your Masculine Energy, work on speaking with confidence and show your competence by doing the analysis, taking action, and focusing on results. By taking small, calculated risks, you'll build courage as you get more by doing more. Everybody wants to work with someone who brings in a project on time and on budget, especially if that proficient person is also caring—a one-two punch that demonstrates the importance of Gender Physics.

Experiment with Body Language

Amy Cuddy, a Harvard Business School professor and social psychologist, delivered a highly acclaimed TED Talk about body language and how it not only affects how others see us but also, more importantly, how we see ourselves. She declares that by faking feelings of power you will actually feel more powerful and advises, "Don't fake it till you make it. Fake it till you become it."

Cuddy conducted research on people in high-power poses, where they sit tall and take up space. She also tested people in low-power poses, where they shrink and hunch over. She proved that in a matter of two minutes, sitting in a high-power pose raised the dominance hormone testosterone and made people more likely to take risks. Likewise, those sitting in the low-power poses developed more of the stress hormone cortisol, which made them more risk averse. In other words, your body can directly affect your mind. In Cuddy's words, "Tiny tweaks can lead to big changes."

If you want to use your body to express Masculine Energy, put your shoulders back, expand your chest, and make yourself bigger. Open your body to take up more space at the table, sitting up straight and erect in your chair. Speak slowly and directly, projecting your voice, and look people in the eye. This is effective in most aspects of business, such as making a sales call, giving a presentation, or asking for a raise. By consciously accessing Masculine Energy, you'll feel and look more confident, and others will have more confidence in you as well.

Those operating within Feminine Energy are conscious of people around them. They avoid invading the space of others or bumping into them on the street. Instead of walking forward in a straight line, expecting others to move, they will anticipate the movements of others and weave around them. They use receptive gestures and inviting smiles. Most of us use Feminine Energy body language when we are speaking to children. If you want to be in their comfort zone and coax a shy little person, you'll want to lower yourself to or beneath their eye level, tilt your head a little to the side, and use a soft voice. This body language was used successfully in the Hollywood cop thrillers of the '80s and '90s. After a brutal interrogation by the 'bad' cop, who in their Masculine Energy Vice would try to intimidate a suspect into giving a confession, the 'good' cop would show up and use a nurturing approach to coax out the information.

You can develop your Masculine Energy by using Masculine body language and Feminine Energy by using Feminine body language. You'll tend to present using the body language of your Go-To Energy, yet you can grow your Complementary Energy based on how you hold your body. Here's a little tip: A good way to use Gender Physics to reach your objectives is to combine Masculine Energy body language (which heightens confidence in your leadership abilities) with some Feminine Energy attributes such as empathy and collaboration to show that you care.

Experiment with Baby-Step Changes

Unlocking the energy you never knew you had to get the results you want will take a bit of finesse. People often recognize the need to make an adjustment, but then overcompensate and swing from one extreme to the other. It takes practice to find balance without going too far in the opposite direction.

Consider a Masculine Energy manager who relishes their position at the top of the hierarchy as the department head and falls into the Vice of being a *dictator*. Staff walking into the weekly department meeting are anxious because the manager's usual pattern is to start by pointing out all the things they did wrong in the previous week. Everyone is on high alert, busy preparing their defense and planning what they will offer to deflect attention from themselves or soften the blow of critical words. However, this time, for this meeting, the manager has decided to try using Feminine Energy.

The manager begins the meeting by looking around the room and asking people to share their 'wins' for the week. Absolutely no one is prepared for this, and team members silently look at one another until a few sputter and spurt out cautious comments. The manager merely sits and listens and does not offer any comments. Eventually, people run out of things to say. The silence is uncomfortable, and everyone leaves the meeting perceiving the new energy of the manager to be passive-aggressive. They whisper and mutter amongst themselves, imagining that the manager has some hidden agenda. Perhaps people are going to be fired, and the manager is looking for points of weakness? Perhaps the manager is being cruel and making the staff squirm first? The staff are confused.

Because no one at the meeting was sharing and everyone seemed withdrawn and uncomfortable, the manager could see that the new approach didn't work and was frustrated. The manager failed to realize that the energy shift was too extreme and failed to consider how that drastic change might be interpreted by others. At this point, many people give up. They identify that they are operating in the Vice of one energy, but they don't grasp that the solution is not to go to the extreme of the opposite energy. Instead, the solution is to inject a small amount of the Complementary Energy, gauge what works, and then dial it up a little further after a few wins.

Overcompensation is a common phenomenon when we are striving for growth. It is natural that when people are trying out a new energy, they tend to insert too much of its Complement. Think of it like a meal you are trying for the first time. Your perception of the meal is that it will be too bland, and you accidentally oversalt it. The result is not very pleasant. The next time you order that meal, you'll remember your mistake from the previous experience and add just a pinch of salt. Not surprisingly, it will be much more enjoyable.

> When trying a new energy, it is best to start with baby steps

Success seldom comes from one big move—it comes from minor yet regular actions over time. In the case of the manager, they could have had a much better meeting by adding just a little Feminine Energy to start. They could have encouraged one person on the team to share a recent win and then asked for more sharing and discussion on how to improve things even more. Success is not totally handing things off (especially without forewarning) *or* assuming total control—rather, it is deftly shifting between the two.

On the positive side, the manager had become aware and had accepted that things needed to change, had done the analysis, and then took a stab at making the adjustment. Hopefully, the manager will assess the situation and recognize the need to take smaller steps at the next meeting. We can all develop our Virtues without swinging too wildly into our Vices.

Experiment with the A+ Energy Model

When I give Gender Physics workshops, I start by having people do the Go-To Energy Evaluation found in Appendix 2. Once they know if their Go-To Energy is Masculine or Feminine, I ask them to get into small groups of three or four people with the same energy. After agreeing on a problem they typically encounter from overuse of their Go-To Energy, they put the A+ Energy Model to work and find balance. It is always interesting to observe the way people of the two different energies approach the model. Those with Feminine Energy take more time as they make sure everyone's views are being considered. And because they love the process, they tend to discuss each aspect of the model. They are more practiced at going inside and are very comfortable with the first three steps of the model. Meanwhile, those with Masculine Energy get right at it and almost dismiss the first three steps. They are more comfortable in the last three steps of the model, as doing analysis and taking action are Masculine Energy attributes. The Masculine Energy people are usually the first ones done as well. I have to remind both groups of people that it is important to do all six steps, as the model is balanced. That means that they will access both sides of themselves as they make their way through it.

If you're ready to examine your current modus operandi, it's time to look at the step-by-step A+ Energy Model. This practical-use outline is meant to guide you as you assess and adjust your Go-To Energy. For both Masculine and Feminine Energy people, the model is the same. Each of you will start the model in your own energy and do the first three stages there (Feminine Energy in black and Masculine in gray). For stages 4 and 5, you'll shift over to your Complementary Energy (black shifts to gray numbers and gray shifts to black numbers) and then come back to your Go-To Energy for stage 6.

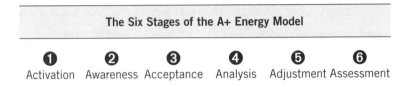

The Six Stages of the A+ Energy Model

❶   ❷   ❸   ❹   ❺   ❻

Activation Awareness Acceptance Analysis Adjustment Assessment

If your preference is for Feminine Energy you will naturally begin there, but once you are activated, become aware, and accept the need for change (first three stages), you'll shift to Masculine Energy and do the next two stages of the energy model, which are analysis and adjustment. Then you'll come back into Feminine Energy to do stage 6 and assess the outcome. If your preference is for Masculine Energy, that is where you will start. You'll do the first three stages there and shift to Feminine Energy for stages 4 and 5. Finally, you'll shift back to Masculine Energy for stage 6.

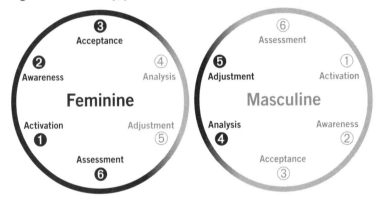

While it may seem like each energy is acting separately from its complement, they are actually interdependent, drawing on the strengths of the other. That compensation and support makes both better together.

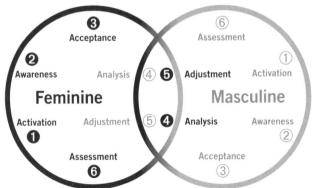

1. **Activation Stage: Reacting instinctively and activating a Go-To Energy response**

Every day we face situations that require our response, and our natural reaction is to turn to our Go-To Energy. It's our comfort zone. Much of the time, it works for us if we use moderation and don't let it get out of hand. However, when we are overtired, overloaded, overwhelmed, uncertain, or stressed—or when we are feeling desperate to change a situation—it is natural to turn to our Go-To Energy and dial it up to the extreme. That's when the Virtues of our Go-To Energy can become Vices. Once we are in the extreme of our Go-to Energy, it is easy to swing to the extreme of our Complementary Energy. This unpredictable seesaw of our imbalance can leave those we interact with confused, uneasy, and often defensive. It can cause communication breakdowns just when we most need good interaction. Unfortunately, it seems that we are often most vulnerable to such a reaction when the stakes are high.

 2. **Awareness Stage: Weighing the advantages and disadvantages of your Go-To Energy style**

Now that you are aware of the Masculine and Feminine Energy attributes, you can consider whether your energy style is providing the results you want. When it's working, feels right, and isn't broken, there's no need to fix it, but you might consider the potential of lost opportunities. Maybe things could be even better? If you are unhappy, unhealthy, or uncomfortable; have an unsettled feeling in your body; or are in a power struggle with another, you are probably out of balance. It is important to stop and take a moment and observe yourself from a distance, as though you are watching the situation on a movie screen. Or doing a high-level scan from 30,000 feet up. This is about stepping back to witness your personal experience objectively. In this state, you are neither stuck in memories of the past nor worrying about what's to come—you are simply noticing. Being in the present moment and practicing awareness allows us to experience the current situation without judgment. This lowers resistance, which improves our understanding and makes us more open. It lays the groundwork for the next stage.

 3. **Acceptance Stage: Recognizing the advantages of adjusting your Go-To Energy**

Rather than accepting things, we can become resistant. This reaction arises from expectations of how we want things to be or what we think they should be. When we allow things to be as they are and recognize that we are 'where we are meant to be,' we have entered the stage of acceptance. This does not mean that we have to like the situation but, rather, that we accept it for what it is. Acceptance releases the pain associated with resistance and opens us up to considering alternatives. This is an important step, as it is an acknowledgment that change would be advantageous.

 4. **Analysis Stage: Considering alternative attributes and solutions**

At this step, Masculine Energy people shift to Feminine Energy to 'try on' those attributes, and Feminine Energy people do the same with Masculine Energy attributes. When doing our analysis, it's important not to beat ourselves up reviewing how we wish we had acted but, rather, consider how to improve our actions and reactions. We may conclude that the energy that gets results at the office can't be applied effectively at home, so the issue is venue. Or we might consider the audience—sometimes the energy that inspires confidence in your boss leaves your subordinates feeling neglected and abused. This insight can help with the right adjustment. Next, it is time to consider the six categories of Variables and decide which one you are in (it could be more than one). Then, notice the Virtue and choose the Vice(s) you wish to adjust. Once you've decided, take some time to analyze how you would feel comfortable expressing the Complementary Energy and visualize that action. Then prepare yourself to shift the energies.

 5. **Adjustment Stage: Adopting the most resonant attribute of your Complementary Energy**

In this step, you shift from your Go-To Energy and insert some of your Complementary Energy. While it sounds simple to make the needed adjustments, it is very personal and, therefore, important to find actions that feel authentic to you. This takes some experimentation and can feel like the 'messy middle,' when things don't seem clear. Stepping from 'known' to 'new' isn't easy, and it can be tempting to throw in the towel. But once the right skills are internalized, it becomes as easy as a golf swing whose movements you've perfected. Eventually, you become adept at shifting back and forth easily and smoothly between the attributes of both energies—you won't have to think about it, you'll just do it.

6. **Assessment Stage: Gauging the success or failure of the experiment**

If you were pleased with the outcome of your energy shift, take notes and/or write down your thoughts about the encounter. Later, you can replay the results mentally to embed the experience in your memory. In the future, when a similar situation arises, you can then access the memory of how you handled it. With time and repetition, accessing those memories and experiences becomes an automatic reflex, until eventually, you shift between your energies instinctively. When you can cite examples of success with the use of a certain energy, you can then recreate those positive results in future situations.

Putting the A+ Energy Model to Use

Implementing the specific steps of this model in strict order can seem cumbersome at first, but by following the steps with discipline, rather than being ambiguous about shifting energies, you'll have more 'Hollywood endings' when practicing Gender Physics. To see how the model works, let's go through the stages using an actual example.

1. **Activation**

Your primary Go-To Energy is Feminine—your inclination is always to agree with others and never say "no." You don't want to disappoint your boss because you want your name to come to mind when the next promotions are being handed out. Also, you have always believed that if you continue to work hard, eventually you will be recognized. Hard work always pays off … right? It's 4 P.M. on a Monday afternoon. You are already under the gun with a critical deadline looming when your boss enters your office and drops several files on your desk, stating, "I need the top one by Wednesday, but the others can wait until Thursday," and then exits without waiting for you to respond. Your instinctive reaction automatically activates your Go-To Energy response, making you want to lead with Feminine Energy. "Sure, give it to me. I'll get it done. No problem."

2. **Awareness**

You sit for a moment staring at the door. You are innately optimistic—but you also realize that you're exhausted and cannot continue looking after the needs of everyone else. You realize that taking on more than you can handle is not doing anybody any good. You haven't been home for dinner in weeks. You're feeling dissatisfied, taken advantage of, even angry—worse, you fear that soon, you will not have the time or ability to do anything well. You observe the situation objectively and realize that what's happening here is not right and it's not working.

3. **Acceptance**

You take a few minutes to reflect: Your boss takes advantage of how accommodating you are. When your boss first started to increase your workload, you were flattered and it was good for your self-confidence ... so you just grinned and said, "You're welcome." You always said "yes" to more work ... even when you couldn't get it done during regular (paid) working hours. Your boss stopped asking if you could take on more work and started just assuming that you would get it done. Coworkers started suggesting that your boss give you assignments that they couldn't fit in (during paid work hours). You shrugged, smiled, and told yourself that each assignment was a good learning opportunity. But you've come to realize that your boss isn't training the rest of the department to do this work—it's easier to download it onto you. Now you work so many evenings and weekends that your family is unhappy. You've started feeling mad at your coworkers and resentful toward your boss. The way you are feeling, working, and reacting is hurting your relationships, and you accept that you have had a big part in creating the situation that you are in today. This releases the frustration and provides you with the ability to analyze how you might change. Congratulations, you are ready to consider the options.

4. **Analysis**

Now, using the Virtues and Vices Reference in Appendix 4, look through the Variable categories to find which ones you are exhibiting. You may find more than one since they are all connected. In this situation, you determine that your inability to say "no" fits under the *Follow/Lead* Variable, and the Virtues *accommodate/assert.* You realize immediately that you have fallen into the Vice of *being a doormat* (too accommodating). Then you ask yourself if there are other applicable Virtues and Vices. You might realize that you are not acting in your own *self-interest* and are being too *other-oriented* from the *We/Me* Variable, as you are certainly in the Vice of *loss of self.* You might say to yourself, "I'm not asserting myself enough. I'm allowing way too much stuff to be piled on me, and I'm becoming submissive. I need to act with more self-interest and establish some boundaries."

5. **Adjustment**

You are now ready to make the adjustment by selecting and adopting the most resonant attribute of your Complementary Energy. It is time to shift. You need to formulate a plan for how to say "no" most effectively. This will take some time, because you need to consider how you will employ this energy attribute that feels new and strange to you. You do some reading and mull over suggestions to see which alternative would feel the most comfortable for you:

a. *Simply say "no"*: You don't need to go into a lengthy explanation—just say, "No, I really can't do that," and stop (remember the *Moneyball* story?). Not saying more is an assertive and very succinct Masculine Energy communication style. You are putting the situation back in the other person's lap so that they can solve the problem themselves.

b. *Make a joke*: "Yeah, I could to do that for you ... Oh! But first I'll need to find a wheelbarrow—because that's what it's going to take to get all the other work off my desk ... but sure, then I'd love to help you with that." Humor can help to defuse a tense situation, but not everyone is comfortable pulling it off.

c. *Offer a choice*: "Yes, I can do that, but here are three other things with similar deadlines. Which one do you want me to drop? Or who would you like me to pass one or all of these along to?"

You might keep using your Feminine Energy—perhaps to find a creative solution to get the work done, such as hiring a contractor. You also might find a solution in one of the other Variables, such as collaboration from the *Build/Win*

Variable, and suggest that you institute a collaborative team approach to get the work completed. Don't forget, though: after you've used your Feminine Energy to come up with a new way of doing things, you'll need to switch over to Masculine Energy to convince others to implement it.

6. **Assessment**

You are now ready to assess the success, or failure, of your experiment and whether adding the Complementary Energy attribute to soften your extreme energy garnered the results you desired. Did you get more of what you wanted? Monitor yourself on an ongoing basis.

A Quick Review

Give me six hours to chop down a tree,
and I will spend the first four sharpening the axe.
—*Abraham Lincoln*

The application of Gender Physics is an ongoing, lifelong experiment, and every situation requires a different energy, and a different amount of it. Sitting in front of you now are all the tools and two questions: What do you do with them? How do you know when to dial your energies up or down? Really, there is no shortcut.

The only way to learn how to bring the right gender energy to any given situation is by turning your career into an experiment. You must become aware of, accept, and analyze the aspects of the behavior that you wish to change … and then you need to develop a plan, seize an opportunity, and adjust.

By embracing Gender Physics, you can ride your bike by pedaling to move forward while making adjustments using the best of each energy's attributes. Instead of leaning too far into either energy and being off balance, you can take your hands off the handlebars and coast down the road of success.

Use Gender Physics to Get Down to Business with This:

- Dial up your Feminine Energy by empathizing and showing others that you care.
- Dial up your Masculine Energy by confidently doing the analysis, taking action, and focusing on results.
- Find common ground with others by looking at the situation from the position of their Go-To Energy.
- Be attentive when trying out a new energy: the tendency is to insert too much, overcompensate, and swing from one extreme to the other.
- Increase your likelihood of successfully using the Complementary Energy by taking baby steps, which are minor yet regular actions over time.
- Develop your Complementary Energy by spending time in homogeneous gendered groups, by implementing appropriate body language, and by experimenting with the A+ Energy Model.

Chapter Ten

Why Gender Physics? Why Me? Why Now?

If nothing exists independent of its relationship to something else,
we can move away from our need to think of things as polar opposites.
—Margaret Wheatley

By using Gender Physics, you will become a more rounded individual and whole human being. You'll be aware of your preference to lead with Masculine or Feminine Energy and cognizant of the importance of inserting some of your Complementary Energy to stay balanced and avoid falling into your Vices. With this, you will be perceived as a caring and confident leader displaying the precious commodity of presence. But to accomplish this, you must get out of your own way and let go of preconceived notions of who you (and the rest of the world) think you should be.

This feat was exemplified in the performances of both Ryan Gosling and Emma Stone in the hit film *La La Land*. Although it is unlikely that either would describe themselves as a singer or dancer, they stepped outside of their comfort zone and, with playful, unapologetic abandon, created something special. It would have been easy for them to self-critique and second-guess themselves. Instead, they left behind their inhibitions and achieved a level of transcendence while we sat transfixed by their presence, transported outside of time and space and into their world.

Magnetism is not reserved for stars of the silver screen alone. It can be found amongst the people that we live and work with— and it can be us! We can achieve the transcendence of Gosling and Stone by leaving behind limiting gender expectations and adopting both interdependent energies. By shifting dynamically between these energies, which shine the brightest together, we'll have the aura and charisma known as presence. But to do that, you must face the fear of not fitting in.

Face the Fear

Many of us have been raised with the notion that the rules of society just are what they are and that challenging them is not only useless but also can hurt our chances of a 'good life.' Any deviance from the norm earns scowls of disapproval on the brows of our seniors. If we want to be with the in-crowd, we have to maintain the expected pose, gesture, and behavior. It's not easy to break our systematic socialization and programming. It can feel like we are in an awful dream walking through our high school naked with everyone looking, judging, and laughing at us.

The worst thing we can do is to work against our own natures, yet many of us do it every day. We do not embrace who we truly are because of fear. Fear of dismissal. Fear of poverty. Fear of losing someone close. Fear of ruining our career. Fear of disappointing our parents, our teachers, and even our children. But how is that serving us?

Fear comes from a lack of knowledge. We fear the dark because we cannot see what is there, and our parasympathetic nervous system activates in order to protect us from danger. This is a primal fear, something wired into every human's psyche, because we have had reason to fear that dark, and those who heed that fear are more likely to survive.

The antidote to the fear of the dark is what? Light, of course. When we shed light on an area and can see that it is clear of danger, we can take a deep breath and relax. Our parasympathetic nervous system then sends out hormones to deactivate the adrenaline in our body so that it returns to a state of homeostasis, or balance.

It would not be fair for me to suggest that you just push past your fear and essentially get over it. The fear is real, and just white-knuckling it to make a change will only increase your anxiety. What can help you escape the burden of your stereotype and get out of your own way is embracing introspection, overcoming doubt, finding support, developing resilience, and cultivating understanding.

Embrace Introspection

We are all of equal worth, and our companies will be most productive if we contribute in our own distinctive and unique way. That starts by becoming self-aware and getting to know yourself as an individual. What are your skills and talents? What makes you feel like a bigger, fuller human being? Activate your Feminine Energy and reflect on this. Then accept what you've learned, and use your Masculine Energy to single-mindedly commit to living that truth.

Some will say, "I know that I'm good at theater, but I want to be an investment banker." That isn't being true to yourself. Play to your strengths. Successful companies know that this is the key to a higher valuation by investors, and you can learn from their experience.

Increasing your self-awareness also comes from focusing on what you value. That takes more introspection. You have already started on this road by reading this book and taking the Go-To Energy Evaluation. You now know whether your natural inclination is to lead with Masculine or Feminine Energy attributes and can see the value in using both. The problem is that, like the rest of us, you have been conditioned to express only the attributes of your biological gender.

What you need now is the conviction to step outside your comfort zone and develop your Complementary Energy. That will allow you to unfold your other wing and fly higher, further, and faster. I can't promise immunity from the cultural backlash that comes when you use the technique of a different gender energy, but I can promise that by following your passion, you'll find the conviction that it is worthwhile.

With meaning, your job can become a calling, inspiring you to scale the steepest cliffs

The conviction to make change comes from knowing what gets you out of bed each day and propels you forward. If you know what you value, your life will have meaning and you'll naturally have more energy. Without meaning, work is a Monday-to-Friday grind. With meaning, your job can become a calling, inspiring you to scale the steepest cliffs.

I've seen this 'transformation to transcendence' time and time again. One woman who values beauty has pursued a career in design. It brings her such joy to share her love with others that she will stay up all night to perfect a project. Interestingly, rather than draining her, the task becomes an all-night energizer.

Another friend, who values adventure, has a successful career as a travel writer. His bags are always packed and his schedule would bury most of his colleagues, but he comes home full of energy and enthusiasm for the new worlds he has just experienced.

Some may value such things as empathy, inventiveness, thrift, or independence. Each case is individual, but all these people are infused with extra energy to advance their goals when working on projects that are meaningful to them. That's when life feels right.

But just because life seems right, that doesn't mean it flows along effortlessly. Quite the contrary. Rejecting the status quo and challenging accepted stereotypes dictates letting go of our Gender Pull, and that can be scary. However, when fear rears its ugly head, our values will provide the conviction and motivation to take action rather than hold back.

For example, meaning can motivate a shy Feminine Energy person who is most comfortable when listening to book a meeting with the CEO and speak convincingly for continuing a program they really believe in. Likewise, an action-oriented Masculine Energy person who values the team will slow down and take time to shed a tear with a colleague who has just lost their mother. We'll never do it for ourselves alone, but we'll risk criticism to change for a meaningful cause.

Overcome Doubt

The fear (darkness) we experience when breaking free of our Gender Pull is unsettling, as we cannot see the outcome, and that can create disaster scenarios in our mind. We have to overcome our doubt by reclaiming our power from the relentless voice in our head. In fact, this action alone may be the biggest single contributor to breaking free of limiting gender stereotypes and expressing yourself as the whole and complete individual that you are. Much like Dorothy in *The Wizard of Oz*, you will find that, though the voice means well, it is actually full of tricks masquerading as the wizard behind the silk curtain.

The voice in your head so badly wants to be the all-knowing wizard that it judges, exaggerates, and takes things personally, all in an effort to control. The sad result is that, instead of enjoying the new office that came with the promotion, the voice is busy pointing out all that is wrong with it. Soon, neither the office nor the promotion feels special at all. Listening to it is not only distracting, but even immobilizing. It is an obvious drag on your daily performance.

With the busy, busy voice talking all time, it is easy to read too much into everything, imagine insults, and become paranoid. Your supervisor doesn't respond to your e-mail because she is in meetings all day. But instead of considering that possibility, the voice announces that she read your e-mail and thought your ideas were stupid. The voice goes on to say that you should have stayed in your Feminine Energy and kept your ideas to yourself.

Now you'll never get anywhere with her as she clearly doesn't like someone who offers unsolicited advice.

This hyperbole continues in its inevitable downward spiral, exaggerated and larger than life until at last the voice arrives at the conclusion that your colleagues probably don't like you either. It then makes the next obvious deduction and suggests that maybe it is time to start looking for another job. All this histrionic confusion from an unanswered e-mail? It is crazy making.

Dealing with the fear of stepping outside gender stereotypes means overcoming the doubts planted by the relentless voice in your head. Consider the following suggestions to deal with it.

1. Script a different story

An accomplished businesswoman and acquaintance described a technique she uses very effectively. She was very passionate about a charitable cause, to which she devoted copious hours and on which she expended huge amounts of energy. While describing the project to her company's CEO, she thought (and the voice in her head concurred) that he rolled his eyes. She was incensed for the remainder of the day, and later that evening, indignantly described the event to her husband. After listening to her retell it, her husband nonchalantly responded with a shrug, "Maybe he just had something in his eye." Upon consideration, she decided that her husband's version was just as likely to be the correct account of the encounter and that the alternative conclusion was not only far more pleasant to believe but also offered great relief. Take a page out of this woman's book. Rather than listening to the negative scenario that comes from the voice in your head, determine to consciously make up a positive story as to why things could be happening the way that they are. For example, perhaps the guy who just cut you off in traffic had to get to the hospital, so there is no need to waste valuable energy being angry at him. Scripting a different story can help prevent you from being triggered and dialing up your energy to the extreme. It just takes a little awareness.

2. **Watch your life from a distance**

   Spiritual gurus suggest that to overcome fears and remain objective, you should observe your life from a distance, as though you were watching the latest film on the silver screen. When shifting energies, look at the situation, contemplate, and try to take it in, without becoming overly involved or attached. It can be very illuminating to recognize that, like a movie, life will happen regardless of what the voice in your head has to say about it. In fact, much as it would have you believe otherwise, the voice has no effect on events that occur in the external world. Instead, take the opportunity to sit back, relax, and eat your popcorn!

3. **Challenge the voice in your head**

   If you listen to what the voice in your head is telling you and find evidence to reinforce the negative comments, a molehill of insecurities will soon grow into a mountain. When the voice accuses you of being stupid and unappealing, reassure it that people are indeed interested in you. Find examples that counteract the assumptions and cite them back to the voice. For example, you might say, "I may not be smart in every department, but we all have strengths and weaknesses. I have a light, and when I let it shine through, I am valuable and appreciated. For example, remember the time when ... [list specific examples]." Just like in real life, if you stand up for yourself and say it with conviction, you'll find inner strength. The voice in your head will be deflated and have no choice but to back down.

When Dorothy painstakingly made her way to the Emerald City and discovered that the great Wizard of Oz was, in fact, a mere mortal, she said, "Oh, you're a very bad man." To which he replied, "Oh no, my dear, I'm a very good man. I'm just a very bad wizard."

You are not the voice in your head any more than the little man was the wizard. The only power the voice has is that which you give it, and there is little benefit from listening to it. Like Dorothy, you will come to realize that you are capable of getting yourself back to Kansas in spite of the voice that tells you it is not possible. Pull back the curtain, take back your power, and give the relentless voice in your head a rest. It will be one of the best things you can ever do to help you overcome the fear of stepping outside your stereotypical gender conditioning. This, in turn, will allow you to become the unique and distinct person that you are.

Find Support

Finding support in life is essential to our human existence; we are social creatures who rely on others to thrive and survive. No man or woman is an island. Sometimes we think we have to do everything all the time and that asking for help or support is a sign of weakness. In truth, it is a sign of strength.

Having others support us, and hold our hand physically or even metaphorically, can give us permission to be brave and help us find the strength to try the cloak of our Complementary

Energy. Imagine that darkness before you and a legion of support-ers shining their lights to guide your way. Surrounding yourself with people who support you is one of the best ways to ensure your success when breaking free of Gender Pull and using both the Feminine and Masculine Energies available to you.

There are a few relationships that can make all the difference to our success and satisfaction. Here are my recommendations.

1. **Secure a mentor**

   This can be a formal or informal association, but it should be with someone you trust. Even better is someone who has been through what you're now experiencing. For example, if you are a Masculine Energy, take-charge kind of person who must learn how to develop your follower-ship to avoid a power struggle with a new boss, it helps to find someone who has had a similar experience. They can provide advice regarding the lay of the land or what could be over the horizon based on what they have been through. Alternatively, spending time with a mentor who leads with your Complementary Energy can help you see the benefits of their approach and encourage you to model their behavior. However, remember that men are expected to act with Masculine Energy attributes and women are expected to display Feminine Energy ones. Men can dial up their Masculine Energy much higher than women with-out people finding it offensive. Thus, if you are a woman adopting the advice of a man to take a hard stand with a coworker, it will serve you well to be cognizant of inserting some Feminine Energy attributes such as empathy or a soft tone of voice when you do it. Each of us has to determine how to adopt our Complement in a way that is right for us individually, but we'll be more motivated to take a risk when we have the benefit of a mentor's expertise. Especially if we have a mentor who inspires us to live a more rewarding and satisfying life by escaping our gender stereotype.

2. **Engage a coach**

    I belong to a few groups of executive women, many of whom are not only coaches themselves but also have their own coaches. This outside perspective helps them walk the narrow minefield of expectations that women face: we are supposed to be strong, tough, and unemotional to be considered good leaders, yet due to unconscious bias, society is suspicious of women with these characteristics. It's no wonder we need some guidance! A coach can help us strategize about our actions and play devil's advocate regarding our plans. They can also be a cheerleader when we need some encouragement (they don't need pom-poms, just enthusiasm for our cause) or an objective listening ear if we throw a pity party. A coach holds space and a process to help you reach a conclusion that is right for you. They don't have to understand Gender Physics, but they will ask insightful questions to make you think. For example, they may ask whether you are sacrificing the building of relationships in order to reach your goals. If you realize that's the case, you'll know that you are too much in your Masculine Energy and that it is time to dial back your focus on outcome and insert some heartfelt Feminine Energy to connect with people.

3. **Establish a personal board**

    This functions much like a business board in that it's meant as a check on performance. I recommend that people build a personal board of four or five people they can reach out to for advice and help to move through difficult situations. While you can meet with them as a group, most often the logistics are too difficult, and meeting individually works just as well. Like a personal coach, the individuals on your board don't have to understand Gender Physics to help you determine which energy to use. Simply describe your problem and your plan to deal with it. You'll get diverse opinions, and that's the beauty of it. After considering all their ideas, you can determine the best action to take. This is especially helpful when considering the alternatives in the fifth—adjustment—stage of the A+ Energy Model. Making the needed adjustments to shift from one energy to another is very individual and can feel uncomfortable; therefore, it is very helpful to have others share their experiences and offer the pros and cons of potential actions. If you talk to your board members about your energy experiment, you might also be surprised by how many of them will be interested in the A+ Energy Model and want to try the experiment right alongside you.

4. **Make friends**

Your network is really your friendship group, and all of us need the support of traveling companions on our journey. These are the people we can turn to when we're frustrated in the office and need to blow off some steam. They are also the ones we can open up to about professional struggles and with whom we can share our vulnerabilities. Their acceptance can help us break through self-imposed limitations and allow us to embrace who we really are. The key is that your friends are positive mirrors for you, reinforcing the truth of who you are deep inside at your core. If it's the

other way around—that is, if you let others define you—
you'll become a poor facsimile of who you really are. No
matter how different you feel, there are people out there
who will reflect back to you the wonderful person that you
are, but you have to find the courage to reveal yourself to
them first. Share this book with them so they can join you
in your energy experiments (and you can return the favor
and be a similar feedback resource to them). It has been
proven that someone who is part of a group, or buddy
system, fares better in lifestyle changes such as losing
weight or carrying on after the death of a loved one. Part of
it is receiving support and part is sharing your objectives
out loud, which makes you more accountable to the group
(and to yourself). Their healthy reinforcement makes it
harder to opt out if we decide to stay in our comfort zone
and not use our Complementary Energy. Also, our best
friends will most likely share our value system, so if we lose
motivation, they can help us find it again by reminding us
what is important. The key is that we don't need to fear
because we are never alone.

Not all support will be in the form of close
friends. You will also need to gain the support of colleagues. In spite of the fact that
we want to be authentic and express our
individuality, it is still important to consider your audience and the culture of your
organization. For example, a good friend, who
is a successful fundraiser, organized an event that
included professional hockey players and coaches. Right away,
she learned that if she wanted to approach them with a request,

Be yourself, but always consider the culture of your audience

she had a much better chance of getting agreement if she called the day after a winning game.

She had never followed the National Hockey League (NHL) before, yet she immediately adapted her personal schedule to that of her audience. Additionally, she peppered her vocabulary with sports metaphors, using language that the players and coaches related to. By making adjustments to her style to match that of her audience, she helped ensure the success of her project.

When developing your network of support, it also helps to consider others' frame of reference. For example, on a construction site, workers will likely expect a boss to exhibit Masculine Energy and be no-nonsense and confident, assigning tasks in an assertive and directive manner. Anything less and you could be considered a wimp, so if you are working in this culture, dial up your Masculine Energy to gain respect. However, if you are working in a primary school, be prepared to dial up your Feminine Energy and gently inquire about others' feelings to show that you care. In such environments, others will expect you to show your soft side, and those that don't will have trouble gaining support.

Geographic regions also lead with Feminine or Masculine Energy

This can be exaggerated even more by geography. I discovered this when traveling back and forth between the US and Canada in my corporate career. For example, both Alberta and Texas have economies based on oil and cattle. In both locations, individuals go out alone to wildcat on the rigs or ride the range. To do their jobs, they must be independent and self-sufficient, which infuses those places with Masculine Energy. Likewise with Toronto and New York. Both are money markets, where people live to work. When people feel that time is money, the culture will be very Masculine Energy and will value productivity, efficiency, and timeliness. In these cultures, people are more direct and have less time for niceties.

In Feminine Energy cultures like Vancouver and California, people work to live. They can hardly wait to get off work to go for a run and enjoy the outdoors. In the fishing and farming areas of both countries (East Coast and Midwest, respectively), you'll find more Feminine Energy, where people developed a culture based on helping others get the crop off or fishing boats in. Paying attention to culture can help you meet people where they are at, which will help you establish a firm footing in your relationships with them.

Regardless, research has proven that the workplace is the best place to start your Gender Physics career experiment. Respondents in a gender study released from Pew Research in December 2017 didn't deviate from traditional expectations for men and women, saying that the genders are very different. Men are tough while women are in touch with their feelings; men are providers while women are nurturers. However, they also said that the workplace is one area in which the sexes are more alike than different. This means that each of us has more latitude at work to step outside our Gender Pull and escape our traditional stereotypes. Once we have practiced in that environment, it will be much easier to take it into other areas of our lives.

Develop Resilience

Resilience, your strong inner core, gives you the conviction to carry on, even when things don't go as planned, and it comes from accepting opportunities and risk. While it is tempting to lie back safely in your socially accepted gender energy, if you want things to be better in the future, you'll need to take a risk and change things in the present. When crossing the threshold to use your Complementary Energy, remember that it is a journey and things can go astray. It is quite natural that you'll face obstacles, and maybe even an unexpected fire-breathing dragon, along the way. But in dealing with these situations, you'll gain resilience and the confidence to pick yourself up and try again.

Consider Luke Skywalker in the movie *Star Wars* when he faced the big dark form of the evil villain Darth Vader. Alone and inexperienced, Skywalker was mocked by Vader for his lack of training in lightsaber combat and could easily have given up. However, after Vader easily pulled the lightsaber out of his hand, Skywalker summoned his inner fortitude. There was no one to depend upon but himself, and he managed to escape from Vader, retrieving his lightsaber as well. With the knowledge that he had handled this situation, Skywalker developed resilience and confidence in his inner core.

When conducting your Gender Physics experiments, accept that things will not always turn out how you would like. Rather than wallowing in self-pity, frame the world positively and push through, putting bad experiences behind you. Use good self-talk, since that will help you handle stress and come back into balance rather than dwelling in negativity. Once you have overcome an obstacle, don't diminish the accomplishment and take it for granted. Congratulate yourself on what you have done and use that experience as a springboard to convince yourself that you can do it again next time.

We can listen to lots of advice, but the rubber hits the road when we are tested. That's when we prove that we are capable of making change for ourselves. Each of us has to recognize opportunities, go for them, and if (or when) one doesn't work out, put it behind us.

To do this, one of the things that I have used successfully is a practice I call "This is who I am; this is what I do." I heard this from a lecturer at Canyon Ranch, a health spa in Tucson, Arizona. The lecturer was an occasional jogger who decided that she wanted to run a marathon. In order to make this a reality, she changed her mindset and visualized herself as if she were already a marathoner. Then she started living her life that way as well.

> To build resilience, establish a mindset for change

When she came home from work and didn't feel like training, she'd simply say to herself: "I'm a marathon runner. This is who I am; this is what I do." With that, she would go out for a jog. When she went out to dinner and was offered dessert, she'd say: "Thanks, but no thanks. It's not who I am. It's not what I do. I am a marathon runner." Having the cake wasn't an option—the decision had already been made. She had established a mindset for change.

There's a reason this is so important: every time you have an argument with yourself, you will lose. It's better to decide to do something and just make it a part of your everyday practice. It removes the argument, making it expected and routine.

So start by telling yourself that you are a balanced human being who uses both Feminine and Masculine Energies and flies on two wings. When it becomes necessary to choose an attribute that is outside the accepted stereotype for your gender, simply say to yourself, "This is who I am; this is what I do."

Cultivate Understanding

As children, we are handed black-and-white sketches of whimsical scenes and a box of colored wax sticks with only one main directive. We are told to "color inside the lines." You may try your hardest, but when you begin coloring, you don't have mastery over the fine motor skills of the small muscles in your fingers, hands, and arms. Your first few attempts are met with smiles and praise, even though you failed to do as instructed. But over time, the expectation of coloring within the lines increases, as does that of choosing the correct colors. Wishing to please your teachers and parents pushes you to continue to work harder to stay within the lines, until you have mastered the skill and have the embedded notion that you must color between the lines now and forevermore.

One year, my daughter gifted me one of those new adult coloring books now available. It is full of fanciful designs. It brought back not only a bit of nostalgia from the times we sat coloring at the dining-room table during her childhood but also memories of the soothing and relaxing feelings that came from coloring. Have you ever seen an adult color outside the lines on purpose in these books?

Try it if you like. You may have this irrational feeling of doing something wrong or naughty. You could then try showing your unorthodox masterpiece to friends and family. If you are silently saying to yourself, "No way," that is because you do not want to embarrass yourself or be ridiculed, or worse, have your effort met with silence and a judging look.

Using your Complementary Energy can feel the same way, and for some of the same reasons. If you were a tomboy like I was, you might have heard from an early age to act more like a lady. Or if you were a guy who enjoyed pursuits usually reserved for girls, you may have heard others suggest that you man up. In either scenario, you were coloring outside the lines, and you carry those lessons learned with you today.

Introspection and awareness allow us to recognize this anxiety and fear for exactly what it is—nothing more than the residual of well-meaning adults attempting to 'help' you by defining your gender role. Consider those adult coloring books for a moment. Back in 2013, if you went to your family and friends with a coloring book picture you created, even with colors neatly contained within the lines, you may have been greeted with laughter, or with concern about whether you bumped your head. Yet today, it is completely normal to own them, and even color your pictures with a group of friends, much like people used to do quilting or knitting together. What happened?

Societal views shifted, and what was once odd or even taboo became trendy and cool. The idea of shifting between Masculine and Feminine Energies, and the focus on what gender is, has become common talk and is in the news every day. There is a multitude of reasons why that shift has occurred, but the important thing to think about is that a light shines in the darkness as we move to break out of the gender molds we have been placed in since birth.

Why Gender Physics Now?

A funny thing happened on the way to writing this book—current events in the world demonstrated for us the principles of Gender Physics. Unchecked systems that are out of balance always topple, and a new, more balanced way of being replaces the old. In the last three months of 2017, you couldn't read the news without seeing some new allegation about a politician, media personality, or celebrity being accused of sexual harassment or abuse.

It started as a hashtag, and by the end of 2017, the story became the biggest and most significant of the year. *Time* magazine featured the silence breakers of the #MeToo movement as their "Person of the Year" and Canadian Press followed suit by naming sexual harassment as the most compelling news story of the year. Pundits on both sides of the border predicted the issue would continue to be one of the most reported.

For far too long, unbalanced men with unbridled power abused their position and fell into the Vice of their Masculine Energy stereotype, dominating and subjugating women with sexual harassment and abuse. They are finally being exposed by women who not only have used the collective power of Feminine Energy under the 'umbrella of solidarity' but also have inserted some Masculine Energy to find their voice. Women formalized the whisper network by speaking out loudly for all to hear. Their fear became fury, and they transferred the shame they carried to where it belongs, firmly with the abusive perpetrators. These men are also being publicly humiliated by a society that is reassessing its assumption that men are above women and just below God in the hierarchy of life.

The us vs them mentality creates a gender seesaw

Until now, we've been conditioned to believe that there is a gap between the two genders and that men are in some way superior to women. As we have learned, gender differences are actually small or close to zero. Yet we are taught that people are either men or women, and we then set the genders up in direct opposition to one another. The us vs them mentality creates a gender seesaw where improvement for one gender creates a loss for the other. Men are naturally reluctant to relinquish their place to the perceived opposition and believe that this gives them the right to discount what women say, objectify them, and treat them as playthings. Most often, these acts and the more horrendous sexual harassment we're hearing about had little to do with sexual fulfillment; it was those men demonstrating that they were in control and had the power.

However, behavioral expectations are changing as the system rebalances itself. Tensions are high and tolerance is low, which is creating new cultural norms. Our society, which used to believe the men and discount the women, has done a flip-flop. The women are now being believed, and sexually assaultive behavior is not being tolerated. The system is still being disrupted so we aren't entirely sure how it will shake out, and there are no straight lines with instructions connecting the dots from A to B to C. However, I see this as an important step to stop pitting one gender against the other, to relax the illusion of Masculine and Feminine roles, and to view women and men as individuals with equal value.

Treating both genders as equals will require some sacrifices. While men will give up their higher position in the hierarchy, it also means that women will give up their claim to have higher emotional intelligence (the ability to identify and manage your own emotions and the emotions of others). Currently, studies (such as one from Korn Ferry in 2016) show that women have more emotional intelligence and are better at using soft skills than men. But like other Masculine and Feminine attributes, this is a result of nurture, not nature. From birth, Western women have held an inferior position in a patriarchal society where most are dependent upon a man for their safety and sustenance. As a result, they have become acutely attuned to what is going on in his mind. I can vouch for this, having worked for nearly three decades in a corporate environment. Underlings spent a good deal of time trying to infer the whims of the king (or CEO), to act upon them, and to curry favor with him.

The workplace will be a huge beneficiary of letting go of the duality of either/or worlds as it will provide a much more cohesive work environment. Traditional management separates things into parts, labels them, and then distributes tasks and assignments. Consequently, organizations operate from within silos: rather than viewing the bottom line and the demands of stakeholders holistically, they compete with each other for funds. It is easy to forget that one part is necessary for the other and there is a short distance between the two. In her book *The Female Advantage*, Sally Helgesen said: "What is needed, then, is leaders who can work against feelings of alienation that affect our institutions, by bridging the gap between the demands of efficiency and the need to nurture the human spirit." The task of efficient production can be contrary to establishing relationships that nurture employees, yet both are needed for a successful operation—so how can we bridge that gap?

> The traits displayed in others and in ourselves are one and the same

I keep hitting home this message, but once again: it comes from integrating the interdependent opposites of the Masculine and Feminine in ourselves. It may be that we cling to duality because it is easier to project our shortcomings onto others and blame them than to do the hard work of solving our own personal problems. This pattern of external castigation rather than internal reflection is evident in countries, companies, communities, and couples. We need to realize that the traits displayed in others and in ourselves are one and the same.

Once we embrace the attributes of the opposite gender in ourselves, it naturally follows that we'll accept them in our neighbor as well. In this state, we will no longer view the behaviors of others as faults but, instead, will see their actions as we would our own. And that will lead to deeper recognition and understanding. We'll find sameness instead of separation.

In William Young's best-selling book *The Shack*, God is an African-American woman who calls herself "Papa" and describes herself this way: "I am neither male nor female, even though both are derived from my nature. If I choose to appear to you as a man or a woman, it's because I love you. For me to appear as a woman and suggest that you call me 'Papa' is simply to mix metaphors, to help you keep from falling so easily back into your religious conditioning."

Finding the Masculine and Feminine Energies in ourselves can help each of us live more peacefully on the inside and more successfully on the outside. Furthermore, it will help us address the increasing tension and polarization in today's world. Seeking similarity rather than separation is a way of reconciling our widely disparate views to find common ground. This can be accomplished with Gender Physics, but it does mean that we must give up antiquated views that the Masculine is in some way superior to the Feminine.

Finding the Value in the Feminine

Like many of us in our production-oriented society, I fell into the trap and was guilty of giving too much credence to Masculine Energy during my career. When conducting sales training years ago, I remember saying, "There are three kinds of people: those who make things happen, those who watch things happen, and those who wonder what happened." My intent was to create self-starters, but by expounding that message, I was encouraging everyone to be the first kind of person, one who lives in their Masculine Energy and makes things happen. And, implicitly, I was denigrating the other two categories of people, implying that they had less value and would never make it in the real world.

Our Masculine Energy strengths, which helped us advance from the industrial age to the technological age, have been dialed up to the extreme and have become weaknesses. People realize that things are out of kilter, and they are losing trust in a system focused only on the endgame with no regard for the constituents. I thought about this at a recent social gathering as I floated from group to group listening to concerns of rising global terrorism, suspicions of unbiased media reports, and fears of populist world leaders who are playing to supporters rather than upholding their nation's laws. To stem deteriorating trust and bring things back into balance, we need to tap into our Feminine Energy. But this will take more respect and appreciation for the Feminine. And this starts with our parenting.

Today, girls are being encouraged to develop both their Masculine and Feminine Energy attributes. To meet the expectations of society, girls are expected to be interested in others and to nurture relationships. Parents then supplement this by enrolling their daughters in sports and by telling them they can be firefighters, surgeons, and astronauts. Girls are given the freedom to mix "thinking" with "feeling," preparing them to be balanced leaders in a modern economy.

Yet, while our daughters are being provided these messages of balance and freedom to express themselves, our sons are too often dissuaded from "feeling their feelings" and pursuing interests that are considered Feminine. There exists societal conditioning that boys are supposed to take action and test boundaries, but they aren't encouraged to pursue the social and interpersonal skills that would equip them to build careers in professions such as nursing, teaching, therapy, medicine, and law, which, according to David Deming, a professor of education and economics at the Kennedy School, are the fastest growing occupations.

Take nursing, for example: it offers men the opportunity to make a difference in the world and do many incredibly 'manly' things (like saving people's lives by dealing with a bullet wound in emergency), yet there are very few male nurses. The problem is that many men can't see themselves working in a nurturing role, are uncomfortable being outnumbered by women, and can't get past the stereotype of Florence Nightingale, the founder of modern nursing. Caring needs to become a gender-neutral concept, and until it does, men will not only miss job opportunities but also miss the chance to have deeply satisfying relationships.

Caring needs to become a gender-neutral concept

When a young boy hears the directive "Be a man," he will usually strive to be a powerful, strong, tough provider who keeps an emotionless stiff upper lip. Most often this means sacrificing their compassion and empathy for others, and this exacerbates the problem. In spite of having minimal differences from their female counterparts, boys are schooled to believe that if they are like a girl, they are less of a man. They are teased, ridiculed, and even punished by peers, parents, and teachers. No wonder those boys become men who avoid all things feminine.

By preventing our sons from becoming whole and complete human beings, parents inadvertently inhibit their employment prospects and limit their ability to relate to the feelings of others. These boys grow up to become leaders without the ability to empathize with their constituencies and, thus, are unable to engender the trust of others. If we want balanced leaders and institutions, we need to cultivate a feminine-positive outlook. Males need to feel free to express themselves using Feminine Energy without fear of recrimination, and females need to see that they aren't considered weak by being a girl. This will only occur when we see both genders as having equal value. My hope is that the stories in this book have increased your appreciation of the Feminine and that you will join me in openly encouraging both men and women to find the balance of using both.

Telling Your Story

In 2016, at the closing session for Womentorship, my mentorship program for women held at the University of Saskatchewan Edwards School of Business, we asked for feedback. One woman told us that it had been tough to develop a relationship with her mentor because it hadn't been established organically.

I could have taken this comment personally, and negatively. I could have internalized it and concluded that my program wasn't working, that the young women were not receiving the full benefit of working with a mentor, and that I was a failure at matching students to mentors. These reactions would have been Vices of Feminine Energy. Alternatively, I could have gone on the offensive and led with an excess of Masculine Energy, making the protégée wrong by reminding her that I had warned participants at the outset that "you don't have to like your mentor to benefit from them."

Instead, I'm happy to report that I used my Complementary Energy and acknowledged that her comments were valid. It can be difficult to hear criticism about something you're deeply vested in. However, because of her feedback, I experimented with new ways to enhance the interaction between the matches. Concluding that we bond with people when we share our stories, I made it my mission to understand the elements of storytelling. I knew that it would be easier for protégées and mentors to find common ground and establish empathy if they heard each other's stories.

Think of a story where you were successful using your Go-To Energy

We integrated storytelling into our professional development program, and the result was a far superior experience for our participants. Today, protégées learn how to use storytelling to promote themselves. We also encourage them to nurture their sense of belonging by establishing common ground with others through storytelling, and we use storytelling to increase resilience by repositioning the story and making up a new ending when things don't go as we had hoped. Thanks to balancing both energies, we have a better program.

I have shared many of my stories throughout this book, and I believe that it will benefit you to tell yours as well. Telling our stories helps us to better understand ourselves and the world around us. Looking at where we have been helps define who we are so that we can decide where we want to go. Telling our stories enlightens us by shining a beacon on our beliefs. It is also beneficial for letting go of the things that no longer serve us. Best of all, stories are the way we can help others. Our looking-in-the-rear-view-mirror perspective can help save them from the school of hard knocks.

Use stories as a place to grow ... to discover what defines you. Storytelling can help you use the revolutionary Gender Physics framework and establish you as one of the leaders desperately needed in our companies and countries. I am looking forward to hearing your story—how you called on your Feminine Energy for inner counsel, to connect with others, and to develop caring relationships while using your Masculine Energy to confidently stand in your power, assert your beliefs, and courageously take action. By unlocking the energy you never knew you had, you can get the results you want.

In Conclusion

By using Gender Physics, we can live our lives as the individuals we were meant to be, free from the limiting subset of attributes deemed appropriate for our gender. To do so, we have to release our Gender Pull, but we'll transcend our conditioning, enjoy authenticity, and be sprinkled with the fairy dust of presence.

As businesses, giving up gender will not only double the talent pool available to us but also mean filling the role with the person whose skills are best suited to the position, thus improving productivity and bottom-line results. As families, Gender

Physics means that men and women can work as partners—sharing the financial burden, managing the home, and handling child care—making them more resilient to the many potholes encountered on the journey of life.

Operating with Masculine Energy confidence and Feminine Energy caring will help each of us gain new insights and keep our Virtues from becoming Vices. Of course, achieving that balance will take experimentation, but the satisfaction of becoming a whole human being living with a greater sense of peace will be well worth it.

In the ancient teachings of the Amazon tribes, great weight was placed on the need for harmony between the Masculine and Feminine forces that exist in all human beings. One of their indigenous leaders, Arkan Lushwala, described it in a Sacred Science Team newsletter this way: "The 'true Feminine' brings a deep wisdom, rooted in trusting one's intuition and heart. It is a passionate, creative, and life-giving force which supports deep heartfelt nurturing of all creation and the passing along of traditions from one generation to the next. The 'true Masculine' is characterized by confidence without arrogance; rational thinking without a need to control; honor without a desire for war. It provides stability, strength, and courage in an ever-shifting world."

Use Gender Physics to stay balanced on the bicycle of life

Let these words guide you as you implement Gender Physics and navigate your way on the bicycle of life. By giving up your focus on gender, you can get down to business and experiment with truly being you!

Glossary

A+ Energy Model: Steps to access your Complementary Energy and practice Gender Physics

career experiment: Trying new things to achieve a different outcome in your career

Complementary Energy: The partner gender energy that makes your Go-To Energy better

Feminine Energy: The energy of caring and collaboration

Gender Physics: The ability to access both Masculine and Feminine Energies and move dynamically between them

Gender Pull: The expected stereotypical attributes of your biological gender

gender shift: Moving from the attribute of one gender energy to the other

Go-To Energy: Your natural energy response to a situation

Masculine Energy: The energy of courage and confidence

tool bag: The Variables and Virtues you can use to handle different situations

Variable: The six categories of gender attributes that are your tools

Vice: When a Virtue is overused

Virtue: When an Energy attribute is used in a healthy amount and an appropriate situation

Appendix 1

Gender Physics Principles: History and Research

Masculine and feminine and their relationship to one another have been studied and discussed throughout history. Many research results reinforce the basic tenets of Gender Physics, and a few are listed below.

1. Gender Physics is based on philosophical principles similar to those described by Tao scholars dating back to 2600 BCE. While the interdependent energies of yin (feminine) and yang (masculine), which translate to "shadow" and "light" respectively, are present throughout nature, nothing was seen to be absolutely yin or absolutely yang, but simply more yin or more yang when compared to something else. Yin and yang are used to describe how seemingly contrary forces are interconnected and complement each other in the natural world.

2. Masculine and Feminine were part of Carl Jung's theories of the anima and the animus, which he considered to be part of the collective unconscious. He believed that there is an inner feminine personality in the unconscious of the male. He called this the anima. Likewise, there is an inner male personality in the unconscious of the female, which he called the animus. Jung believed that the overriding goal of individuals was integration. Gender Physics is designed to help you do exactly that: integrate your energies.

3. A 1973 article by Vassar College psychologist Anne Constantinople revolutionized attitudes toward traditional masculine and feminine by proclaiming that the two genders were not at opposite ends of a continuum but rather independent constructs. This gave rise to androgyny theory and the Bem Sex-Role Inventory, which advanced the proposition that individuals could be both masculine and feminine and that, in fact, the healthiest gender orientation was one containing elements of both.

4. Research released by Anne Grethe Solberg of the BI Norwegian School of Management demonstrates that many individuals who reach top levels in the corporate world are androgynous in that they exhibit both feminine and masculine gender role identities. She concluded that this dual leadership style creates the best climate for growth and innovation because it fosters good human relationships, which in turn motivates followers to stretch beyond their job descriptions.

5. Mihaly Csikszentmihalyi, widely recognized as the world's leading researcher on positive psychology, interviewed ninety-one people considered highly creative and concluded that much of their success stemmed from using the attributes of both genders. By using the feminine attribute of sensitivity, these successful individuals were more attuned to subtle aspects of the environment that many would dismiss as unimportant. After recognizing these subtle aspects, the participants then used the masculine attribute of assertiveness to confidently develop and present their work.

6. Dutch anthropologist Geert Hofstede developed a grid for defining masculine and feminine cultures around the world. When determining masculine cultures, he considers several attributes, such as how hierarchical or assertive the society is; Japan and Germany number in the highly masculine category. At the other end of the grid are societies that are very cooperative, which he describes as being more feminine; Sweden is such a culture.

Appendix 2

Go-To Energy Evaluation

As you respond to the following statements, imagine that you are on vacation, not influenced by internal or external expectations of who you should be or how you should perform. In order to get a clear understanding of your natural Go-To Energy, try not to second-guess your responses.

Part 1

Read each statement and choose the word that best applies to you. Record the corresponding score in the space provided.

Never = 1   Seldom = 2   Sometimes = 3   Often = 4   Always = 5

1. I consider others' needs before my own   _____

2. I prefer to reach a decision by group consensus   _____

3. I find the courage to do for others what I cannot do for myself   _____

4. I am energized by the harmony of the group   _____

5. I like to join organizations that are inclusive
   of everyone   _____

6. I don't have to take the lead and trust others
   to direct the action   _____

7. I support others' rights to their opinions, even
   if I disagree with them   _____

8. I find it easy to accommodate others' eccentricities   _____

9. I like to ask questions to learn about others'
   hopes and dreams   _____

10. I listen more than I talk when in a conversation   _____

11. I like to contribute and have others build
    on my ideas   _____

12 I go out of my way to make a relationship work   _____

13. I am a good delegator   _____

14. I seek common ground to make allies out of others   _____

15. I consider the big picture and long-term ramifications
    when taking action   _____

16. I am adept at handling multiple things at once   _____

17. I like to start a project without a plan and see
    where it takes me   _____

18. I enjoy the creative process and have lots of ideas   _____

19. I want contingency plans for potential upsets   _____

20. I try to consider everyone who will be impacted
    when taking action   _____

21. I experience others' pain when I hear about
    their problems   _____

22. I use my intuition for guidance _____

23. I relate to people through shared emotion _____

24. I can see connections between seemingly
    unrelated events _____

25. I feel emotions on a deep level _____

26. I see the complexity and shades of gray in issues _____

27. I am known for my ability to relax _____

28. I pause and reflect before taking action _____

29. I like to take time to imagine "what if?" _____

30. I immediately consider what I could do differently
    when things don't go well _____

Add up all your scores. Write your total here: _____.
Now go to part 2.

Part 2

Read each statement and choose the word that best applies to
you. Record the corresponding score in the space provided.

Never = 1   Seldom = 2   Sometimes = 3   Often = 4   Always = 5

1. I prefer to take care of myself without help
   from others _____

2. I will pay extra for VIP treatment _____

3. I make my own decisions based on my own
   well-being _____

4. I want to be perceived as competent _____

5. I want to stand out from the group _____

6. I like to direct the action when working in a group ____

7. I am vigilant about protecting my property ____

8. I establish boundaries easily by saying "no" ____

9. I stand up for my rights, even when the costs are high ____

10. I have many opinions and like to explain them
    to others ____

11. I consider competition a motivator ____

12. I believe in the value of the hierarchy ____

13. I'd rather play the game than protect the relationship ____

14. I like to see immediate results on projects ____

15. I believe an organization needs a strong, centralized
    structure ____

16. I am more interested in things than in people ____

17. I always consider the end result ____

18. I enjoy setting goals and meeting deadlines ____

19. I don't worry about things that might not happen ____

20. I thrive on my career and live to work ____

21. I only believe in physical things you can see, feel,
    or touch ____

22. I think facts are more persuasive than a story ____

23. I rely on logical analysis as the primary driver
    when making a decision ____

24. I thrive on a good debate ____

25. I base my decisions on cause and effect ____

26. I connect with people by doing an activity with them ____

27. I make things happen   _____

28. I measure my self-worth by my accomplishments   _____

29. I am a risk-taker by nature   _____

30. I like to break things down to a simple format   _____

Add up all your scores. Write your total here: _____.

What Is Your Go-To Energy?

Compare your total scores in parts 1 and 2. If your score was higher in part 1, your natural approach to life is Feminine Energy. If your score was higher in part 2, your Go-To Energy is Masculine Energy.

Most people want to put their scores in context and compare them to those of others, but what is most important is understanding your preference. Know as well that you will be influenced by your own perception of the energies, which can change as your circumstances and experiences change.

You may also find it revealing to look at the statements where you scored either a 1 or a 5. These are the things that you never do or always do. Consider situations such as these where it might be useful to dial up your energy or dial it down. For example, if you are never delegating and always directing, it might be difficult for your team to learn how to make decisions themselves and thus become self-reliant or proficient. You may want to consider handing over some of those tasks on future projects.

Once you have completed this assessment, return to the chapters and look at how your scores line up with particular Virtues to gain better insight into your Go-To Energy.

Appendix 3

Energy Virtues (Strengths)

Feminine Virtues (Strengths)	Masculine Virtues (Strengths)
Collective	Individual
Integration	Differentiation
Inclusive	Exclusive
Other-oriented	Self-interest
Consensus	Autonomy
Listen	Speak
Accommodate	Assert
Pull	Push
Support	Direct
Allow	Establish boundaries
Flat structure	Hierarchical structure
Collaboration	Competition
Relationships	Results
Long term	Short term
Empower	Command and control
Process	Goal
Exercise	Outcome
Problem prevention	Problem resolution
Journey	Destination
Stakeholder	Bottom line
Intuition	Analysis

Feminine Virtues (Strengths)	Masculine Virtues (Strengths)
Emotion	Logic
Empathetic	Rational
Right brain	Left brain
Feeling	Thinking
Reflection	Action
Dream	Achieve
Being	Doing
Respond	Advance
Nuance	Simplification

Appendix 4

Virtues and Vices Reference by Variable

We/Me Virtues and Vices

Virtue Feminine	Vice Feminine	Virtue Masculine	Vice Masculine
Collective	Cult	Individual	Narcissism
Integration	Herding	Differentiation	Segregation
Inclusive	Homogenization	Exclusive	Prejudice
Other-oriented	Loss of self	Self-interest	Egocentric
Consensus	Dependency	Autonomy	Disconnected

Follow/Lead Virtues and Vices

Virtue Feminine	Vice Feminine	Virtue Masculine	Vice Masculine
Listen	Cave in	Speak	Monopolize
Accommodate	Doormat	Assert	Aggressive
Pull	Absorb	Push	Thwart
Support	Placate	Direct	Dominate
Allow	Submissive	Establish boundaries	Subjugate

Build/Win Virtues and Vices

Virtue Feminine	Vice Feminine	Virtue Masculine	Vice Masculine
Flat structure	Confusion	Hierarchical structure	Dictatorship
Collaboration	Demoralized	Competition	Combative
Relationships	Needy	Results	Oppressive
Long term	Disoriented	Short term	Addicted
Empower	Enable	Command and control	Overbearing

How/What Virtues and Vices

Virtue Feminine	Vice Feminine	Virtue Masculine	Vice Masculine
Process	Overwhelm	Goal	Obsess
Exercise	Exhaustion	Outcome	Emptiness
Problem prevention	Paranoia	Problem resolution	Quick fix
Journey	Procrastination	Destination	Impatience
Stakeholder	Martyr	Bottom line	Immoral

Heart/Head Virtues and Vices

Virtue Feminine	Vice Feminine	Virtue Masculine	Vice Masculine
Intuition	Impulsiveness	Analysis	Scrutiny
Emotion	Overdramatic	Logic	Rigid
Empathetic	People-pleaser	Rational	Disdainful
Right brain	Overstimulation	Left brain	Compartmentalization
Feeling	Overreacting	Thinking	Robotic

Know/Go Virtues and Vices

Virtue Feminine	Vice Feminine	Virtue Masculine	Vice Masculine
Reflection	Perfectionism	Action	Recklessness
Dream	Fool's paradise	Achieve	Overambitious
Being	Disengaged	Doing	Compulsive
Respond	Paralysis	Advance	Overreaching
Nuance	Irrelevancy	Simplification	Distortion

Sources

Chapter 1

Joel, Daphna, and others. "Sex Beyond the Genitalia: The Human Brain Mosaic." *Proceedings of the National Academy of Sciences of the United States of America*, December 15, 2015. 112 (50) 15468–15473; published ahead of print November 30, 2015. *https://doi.org/10.1073/pnas.1509654112.*

Williams, Rhiannon. "Facebook's 71 Gender Options Come to UK Users," *The Telegraph*, June 27, 2014. *www.telegraph.co.uk/technology/facebook/10930654/Facebooks-71-gender-options-come-to-UK-users.html.*

Staff writer. "58 Gender Options Not Enough? Facebook Now Allows Unlimited Custom Identities," RT.com, February 27, 2015. *www.rt.com/usa/236283-facebook-gender-custom-choice.*

Lera Boroditsky. "How Does Our Language Shape the Way We Think?" *Edge*, June 11, 2009. *www.edge.org/conversation/lera_boroditsky-how-does-our-language-shape-the-way-we-think.*

Jung, Kiju, and others. "Female Hurricanes Are Deadlier Than Male Hurricanes." *Proceedings of the National Academy of Sciences of the United States of America*, June 17, 2014. 111 (24) 8782–8787; published ahead of print June 2, 2014. *https://doi.org/10.1073/pnas.1402786111.*

Bargh, John. *Before You Know It: The Unconscious Reasons We Do What We Do.* New York City: Touchstone, 2017. Kindle e-book.

"John A. Bargh." Social Psychology Network. *http://bargh.socialpsychology.org.*

Wessel, Jennifer L., and others. "Should Women Applicants 'Man Up' for Traditionally Masculine Fields?" *Psychology of Women Quarterly*, July 25, 2014. *http://journals.sagepub.com/doi/ abs/10.1177/0361684314543265.*

O'Neill, Olivia A., and Charles A. O'Reilly. "Reducing the Backlash Effect: Self-monitoring and Women's Promotions," *Journal of Occupational and Organizational Psychology*, vol. 84, no. 4 (December 2011). *https://doi.org/10.1111/j.2044-8325.2010.02008.x.*

Ehrenreich, Barbara. "The Future of Work: Divisions of Labor," *The New York Times Magazine*, February 23, 2017. *www.nytimes.com/issue/ magazine/2017/02/24/magazine-index-20170226.*

Rosin, Hanna. "The End of Men," *The Atlantic*, July/August 2010. *www.theatlantic.com/magazine/archive/2010/07/the-end-of-men/308135.*

Chapter 2

"Edith Has Jury Duty," *All in the Family*, TV series. IMDb Quotes. *www.imdb.com/title/tt0509851/quotes.*

Burrough, Brian, and John Helyar. *Barbarians at the Gate: The Fall of RJR Nabisco*. New York City: HarperBusiness, 2009.

Chapter 3

Maccoby, Michael. "Narcissistic Leaders: The Incredible Pros, the Inevitable Cons," *Harvard Business Review*, January 2004. *https://hbr. org/2004/01/narcissistic-leaders-the-incredible-pros-the-inevitable-cons.*

"Steve Jobs. "Biography.com. *www.biography.com/people/ steve-jobs-9354805.*

Steve Jobs at Macworld Expo, Boston, August 6, 1997. YouTube, published March 6, 2006. *www.youtube.com/watch?v=PEHNrqPkefI.*

Ali Baba Bunny, Merrie Melodies animated cartoon series. Directed by Chuck Jones. Hollywood: Warner Bros., 1957. *www.youtube.com/watch?v=t8x3vymEWfg.*

Chapter 4

Kelley, Robert. "In Praise of Followers," *Harvard Business Review,* November 1988. *https://hbr.org/1988/11/in-praise-of-followers.*

Copp, Trevor, and Jeff Fox. "Ballroom Dance That Breaks Gender Roles." TED Talks, TEDxMontreal, November 2015. *www.ted.com/ talks/trevor_copp_jeff_fox_ballroom_dance_that_breaks_gender_roles.*

Klein, Ezra. "Understanding Hillary: Why the Clinton American Sees Isn't the Clinton Colleagues Know," Vox, July 11, 2016. *www.vox. com/a/hillary-clinton-interview/the-gap-listener-leadership-quality.*

Farrow, Ronan. "From Aggressive Overtures to Sexual Assault: Harvey Weinstein's Accusers Tell Their Stories," *The New Yorker,* October 23, 2017. *www.newyorker.com/news/news-desk/ from-aggressive-overtures-to-sexual-assault-harvey-weinsteins-accusers-tell-their-stories.*

Staff writer. "Harvey Weinstein Timeline: How the Scandal Unfolded," BBC News, May 25, 2018. *www.bbc.com/news/ entertainment-arts-41594672.*

Desta, Yohana, and Hillary Busis. "These Are the Women Who Have Accused Harvey Weinstein of Sexual Harassment and Assault," *Vanity Fair,* October 12, 2017. *www.vanityfair.com/hollywood/2017/10/ harvey-weinstein-accusers-sexual-harassment-assault-rose-mc-gowan-ashley-judd-gwyneth-paltrow.*

Chapter 5

Tabor, Glenna. "Crab Bucket Mentality." *https://glennatabor.com/ motivation/crab-bucket-mentality.*

Elmer-Dewitt, Philip. "Take a Trip into the Future on the Electronic Superhighway"; cover: "The Info Highway," *Time,* vol. 141, no. 15 (April 12, 1993). *http://content.time.com/time/maga-zine/0,9263,7601930412,00.html.*

Popik, Barry. "Be Nice to People on Your Way Up Because You'll Meet the Same People on Your Way Down," The Big Apple, December 16, 2014. *www.barrypopik.com/index.php/new_york_city/entry/ be_nice_to_people_on_your_way_up.*

Mui, Yian Q. "The World's Tallest Buildings May Come with a Curse," *The Washington Post,* January 12, 2016. *www.washingtonpost.com/ news/wonk/wp/2016/01/12/the-worlds-tallest-buildings-may-come-with-a-curse/?noredirect=on&utm_term=.5fa8a5be7560.*

Hidden Figures, film. Directed by Theodore Melfi. Los Angeles: Fox 2000 Pictures, 2016.

Lyon, Peter. "The Supra Is Back, but This Time It's a Toyota-BMW Collaboration," *Forbes,* January 26, 2018. *www.forbes.com/sites/ peterlyon/2018/01/26/the-supra-is-back-but-this-time-its-a-toyota-bmw-collaboration/#3e7cdeec2001.*

Akwei, Ismail. "Rwanda Tops UN List of Countries with Most Women in Parliament," africanews. com, July 10, 2017. *www.africanews.com/2017/07/10/ rwanda-tops-un-list-of-countries-with-most-women-in-parliament.*

Covey, Stephen R. *The 7 Habits of Highly Effective People: Powerful Lessons in Personal Change.* New York City: Simon & Schuster, 2013. (I purchased this book on its original printing in 1989.)

Chapter 6

Kotter, John P. *Force for Change: How Leadership Differs from Management.* New York City: Free Press, 2008. Kindle e-book.

Moneyball, film. Directed by Bennett Miller. Culver City, CA: Columbia Pictures Industries, Inc., 2011.

The Big Short, film. Directed by Adam McKay. Beverly Hills, CA: Plan B Entertainment, 2015.

Chapter 7

Pink, Daniel H. *A Whole New Mind: Why Right-Brainers Will Rule the Future*. New York City: Riverhead Books, 2006.

Pearsall, Paul. *The Heart's Code: Tapping the Wisdom and Power of Our Heart Energy*. New York City: Harmony Books, 1999.

Nemy, Enid. "Leona Helmsley, Hotel Queen, Dies at 87," *The New York Times*, August 20, 2007. *www.nytimes.com/2007/08/20/nyregion/20cnd-helmsley.html*.

Bolte Taylor, Jill. *My Stroke of Insight: A Brain Scientist's Personal Journey*. New York City: Viking Press, 2008.

Confino, Jo. "How Women Became Stars in the Battle Against Climate Change," *HuffPost*, January 28, 2016. *www.huffingtonpost.ca/entry/how-love-really-did-change-the-course-of-history_us_56a8b7a7e-4b0f7179928722d*.

Chapter 8

Queen Elizabeth I. Speech at Tilbury Camp, July 1588. *www.bl.uk/learning/timeline/item102878.html*.

Baker, Dan, and Cameron Stauth. *What Happy People Know: How the New Science of Happiness Can Change Your Life for the Better*. New York City: St. Martin's Griffin, 2004.

"Julia Levy." science.ca, October 2, 2011. *www.science.ca/scientists/scientistprofile.php?pID=12&pg=3*.

Venkitaraman, Ashok R., and others. "The Seroepidemiology of Infection Due to Epstein-Barr Virus in Southern India," *Journal of Medical Virology*, January 1985. *https://doi.org/10.1002/jmv.1890150103*.

Mandell, Andrea. "Michelle Williams, Mark Wahlberg Reshot Kevin Spacey's 'All the Money' Scenes for Free," *USA Today*, December 19, 2017. *www.usatoday.com/story/life/movies/2017/12/19/michelle-williams-mark-wahlberg-reshot-kevin-spaceys-all-money-scenes-free/966670001*.

Tatna, Meher. "Reshooting 22 Scenes in 9 Days No Problem for Director Ridley Scott," *The Newspaper*, January 24, 2018. *www.tnp.sg/entertainment/movies/reshooting-22-scenes-9-days-no-problem-director-ridley-scott.*

Lauzen, Martha M. "The Celluloid Ceiling: Behind-the-Scenes Employment of Women on the Top 100, 250, and 500 Films of 2017," study, 2018. *https://womenintvfilm.sdsu.edu/wp-content/uploads/2018/01/2017_Celluloid_Ceiling_Report.pdf.*

"Statistics" Women and Hollywood. *https://womenandhollywood.com/resources/statistics.*

McGilchrist, Iain. *The Master and His Emissary: The Divided Brain and the Making of the Western World.* New Haven, CT: Yale University Press, 2012.

Donnie Brasco, film. Directed by Mike Newell, 1997. Los Angeles, CA: Mandalay Entertainment.

Einstein, A. *The Ultimate Quotable Einstein.* Edited by Alice Calaprice. Princeton, NJ: Princeton University Press, 2010.

Chapter 9

Bryant, Adam. "When You Write a Report Card, Explain the Grades," *The New York Times*, June 9, 2012. *www.nytimes.com/2012/06/10/business/laura-yecies-of-sugarsync-on-thoughtful-evaluations.html.*

Johnson, Barry. *Polarity Management: Identifying and Managing Unsolvable Problems.* Amherst, ME: HRD Press, 2014.

Collins, Jim. *From Good to Great: Why Some Companies Make the Leap … And Others Don't.* New York City: Harper Business, 2001.

Cuddy, Amy. "Your Body Language May Shape Who You Are." TED Talks, TEDGlobal 2012, June 2012.

Chapter 10

La La Land, film. Directed by Damien Chazelle. Santa Monica, CA: Summit Entertainment, 2016.

The Wizard of Oz, film. Directed by Victor Fleming. Beverly Hills: Metro-Goldwyn-Mayer Studios Inc., 1939.

Parker, Kim, Juliana Horowitz, and Renee Stepler. *On Gender Differences, No Consensus on Nature vs. Nurture.* Pew Research Center, December 2017. *http://assets.pewresearch.org/wp-content/ uploads/sites/3/2017/12/05142916/Gender-report-December-2017- FINAL.pdf.*

Star Wars, film. Directed by George Lucas. San Francisco: Lucasfilm, 1977.

Zacharek, Stephanie, Eliana Dockterman, and Haley Sweetland Edwards. "The Silence Breakers"; cover: Person of the Year. *Time*, December 18, 2017. *http://time.com/ time-person-of-the-year-2017-silence-breakers.*

Canadian Press: Paola Loriggio. "Sexual Harassment Named Canadian Press News Story of the Year," National Newswatch, December 20, 2017. *www.nationalnewswatch.com/2017/12/20/ sexual-harassment-named-canadian-press-news-story-of-the-year/#. WxMpRxkh1FQ.*

Korn Ferry Hay Group. *New Research Shows Women Are Better at Using Soft Skills Crucial for Effective Leadership and Superior Business Performance.* Los Angeles: Korn Ferry, March 4, 2016. *www.kornferry. com/press/new-research-shows-women-are-better-at-using-soft-skills- crucial-for-effective-leadership.*

Helgesen, Sally. *The Female Advantage: Women's Ways of Leadership.* New York City: Doubleday Business, 1990.

Young, William P. *The Shack.* Winnipeg, MB: Word Alive Press, 2008.

Deming, David J. "The Growing Importance of Social Skills in the Labor Market," *The Quarterly Journal of Economics*, vol. 132, no. 4 (November 1, 2017). *https://doi.org/10.1093/qje/qjx022.*

The Betty-Ann Heggie Womentorship Program, Edwards School of Business, University of Saskatchewan. *www.edwards.usask.ca/womentorship/index.aspx.*

Polizzi, Nick, ed. Sacred Science Team newsletter, March 19, 2016.

Bem, Sandra L. "The Measurement of Psychological Androgyny," *Journal of Consulting and Clinical Psychology*, vol. 42, no. 2 (1974). *http://dx.doi.org/10.1037/h0036215.*

Appendix 1

Heider, John. *The Tao of Leadership: Lao Tzu's Tao Te Ching Adapted for a New Age*. Palm Beach, FL: Green Dragon Books, 1992.

Hill, Gareth S. *Masculine and Feminine: The Natural Flow of Opposites in the Psyche*. Boulder, CO: Shambhala Publications, 1992.

Constantinople, Anne. "Masculinity-Femininity: An Exception to a Famous Dictum?" *Psychological Bulletin*, vol. 80, no. 5 (1973). *http://dx.doi.org/10.1037/h0035334.*

Solberg, Anne Grethe. "Androgenous Leaders Mean Increased Innovation," BI Norwegian Business School, November 6, 2008. Based on lecture "Innovation Leadership in the Boardroom" given at the Norwegian School of Management, October 16, 2008. *www.bi.edu/about-bi/news/2008/11/Androgynous-leaders-mean-increased-innovation.*

Csikszentmihalyi, Mihaly. *Creativity: The Psychology of Discovery and Invention*. New York City: HarperCollins, 1996.

Pogosyan, Marianna. "Geert Hofstede: A Conversation about Culture," *Psychology Today*, February 21, 2017. *www.psychologytoday.com/ca/blog/between-cultures/201702/geert-hofstede-conversation-about-culture.*

General Reading

Banaji, Mahzarin R. *Blindspot: Hidden Biases of Good People*. New York City: Delacorte Press, 2013.

Bhat, Nilima, and Raj Sisodia. *Shakti Leadership: Embracing Feminine and Masculine Power in Business*. Oakland, CA: Berrett-Koehler Publishers, Inc., 2016. Kindle e-book.

Cohen, Martin. *Gender Balancing: An Evolutionary Model for Elevating Relationship from Mediocre to EXTRAORDINARY*. Bloomington, IN: Balboa Press, 2016. Kindle e-book.

Copprue, Tanya. *The Secret of the Masculine & Feminine Energies: A Guide to Healing Relationships*. N.p.: Soul de Diva Press, 2010.

Delee Fromm Consulting Inc. *Understanding Gender at Work: How to Use, Lose and Expose Blind Spots for Career Success*. Victoria, BC: Tellwell Talent, 2017.

Eisler, Riane. *The Chalice & the Blade: Our History, Our Future*. New York City: HarperCollins, 1988.

Fine, Cordelia. *Delusions of Gender: How Our Minds, Society, and Neurosexism Create Difference*. New York City: W.W. Norton, 2011.

Fine, Cordelia. *Testosterone Rex: Myths of Sex, Science, and Society*. New York City: W.W. Norton, 2017.

Foley, Brendan. *The Yin Yang Complex: Create Success by Understanding the World's Oldest Dynamic Forces*. Blackrock, Ireland: Mercier Press, 2010. Kindle e-book.

Goldsmith, Marshall, with Mark Reiter. *What Got You Here Won't Get You There: How Successful People Become Even More Successful*. New York City: Hachette Books, 2007. Kindle e-book.

Grant, Adam M. *Give and Take: Why Helping Others Drives Our Success.* New York City: Viking Penguin, 2013. Kindle e-book.

Jung, Carl G., and others. *Man and His Symbols.* New York City: Dell, 1968.

Kay, Katty, and Claire Shipman. *The Confidence Code: The Science and Art of Self-Assurance—What Women Should Know.* New York City: HarperBusiness, 2014. Kindle e-book.

Kazdin, Alan E. *Behavior Modification in Applied Settings,* 7th ed. Long Grove, IL: Waveland Press Inc., 2012.

Kennedy, Diane. *Yin, Yang and You: The Forces of Co-Creation.* Scottsdale, AZ: LP Publications, 2010.

Kim, Joseph K., and David S. Lee. *Yin and Yang of Life: Understanding the Universal Nature of Change.* N.p.: Heal and Soul, LLC., 2010

Miley, Jeanie. *Joining Forces: Balancing Masculine and Feminine.* Macon, GA: Smyth & Helwys Publishing, 2012.

Myers, Jack. *The Future of Men: Men on Trial.* San Francisco: Inkshares, Inc., 2016. Kindle e-book.

Palmer, Martin. *Yin & Yang: Understanding the Chinese Philosophy of Opposites and How to Apply It to Your Everyday Life.* Essex, UK: Piatkus Books Ltd., 1998.

Smith, Paul. *Lead with a Story: A Guide to Crafting Business Narratives That Captivate, Convince, and Inspire.* New York City: AMACOM, 2012.

Turner, Caroline. *Difference Works: Improving Retention, Productivity and Profitability through Inclusion.* Austin, TX: Live Oak Book Company, 2012.

van der Steur, John. *The Power of Polarities: An Innovative Method to Transform Individuals, Teams, and Organizations. Based on Carl Jung's Theory of the Personality.* Austin, TX: Polarity Institute, 2017. Kindle e-book.

Vedantam, Shankar. *The Hidden Brain: How Our Unconscious Minds Elect Presidents, Control Markets, Wage Wars, and Save Our Lives*. New York City: Spiegel & Grau, 2010.

Wittenberg-Cox, Avivah. *Seven Steps to Leading a Gender-Balanced Business*. Boston: Harvard Business Review Press, 2014. Kindle e-book.

Index

About the Author

Betty-Ann Heggie, a thought leader in gender dynamics, has had articles featured in Inc., HuffPost, Apple News, and The Good Men Project. An award-winning speaker, author, and mentor, she is also a corporate director, a philanthropist, and a former senior vice-president with PotashCorp (now Nutrien), the world's largest fertilizer supplier.

Betty-Ann has been inducted into the WXN Hall of Fame, in recognition of her multiple Canada's Most Powerful Women: Top 100 awards, and the Saskatchewan Business Hall of Fame; has received the Women in Mining Canada Trailblazer Award; and was named one of the 100 Global Inspirational Women in Mining. Other awards include the Queen's Golden Jubilee Medal, the YWCA Lifetime Achievement Award, and the University of Saskatchewan Alumni Mentorship Award. Betty-Ann currently serves on the board of TIFF (Toronto International Film Festival), and she spearheaded the Betty-Ann Heggie Womentorship program at the University of Saskatchewan Edwards School of Business, which has had more than 1,800 women participate in its programs.

More Advance Praise for *Gender Physics*

"If you want to take your career to another level, you'll find Betty-Ann's stories and process extremely practical and enormously inspiring. I wish I'd read this book early in my career; now I'm excited about constructing a workshop based on her work. Breaking out of the duality of gender roles — the belief that we have to be just one or the other — is an idea whose time has come. By moving beyond "he" and "she," we'll see ourselves as 'different and broader expressions of the same,' which will reduce divisiveness and enable us to find common ground."

—**Rox Bartel**, CBHS, ImpactBank

"What a joy it has been to read this book, to journey within its pages toward insight. Brimming with intelligence, philosophy, research, personal story-telling, exercises, and helpful tools, Betty-Ann encourages her readers to consider a next evolution — a full integration of both Feminine and Masculine Energies, molding to situations for best outcomes and toward a rewarding life of successful relationships, empowerment, and toward goals reached. A must-read for anyone wishing to realize their best selves, and especially so for those aspiring to lead with greatest success. Understanding and knowing self is a critical foundation for realizing a purposeful and meaningful life, and by cultivating the best of our Masculine and Feminine Energies, we nurture and grow within our greatest potential. Let the journey begin."

—**Silvia L. Martini**, C.Dir., EBAC, BAC, Entrepreneur, mentor, coach, leader, mother, life partner, volunteer, friend, speaker, writer, and empowerment advocate

"Humanity is moving beyond our old stereotypes. We are limited only by our own misconceptions of our individual gender. Using *Gender Physics* places us beyond the stereotypes and even unconscious prejudices that still exists. Betty-Ann offers a brilliant perspective of allowing a truly complete expression of ourselves."

—**Jacob Lay**, Co-founder, Motus Training Studio, Training in Power Faculty

"The development of leaders is critical to create the workplace culture that will engage employees and maximize the success of an organization. The *Gender Physics* theory provides a model to bring out the best in others as well as ourselves. Organizations, large or small, that want a competitive advantage will invest in learning and applying the principles of this book."

—**Andrea Hansen**, Business Advisor, Partner, Sutton Financial Group

"This book sparked my desire to learn how the ancient knowledge of *Gender Physics* can be a framework to help create a greater balance in life. Betty-Ann uses a writing style rich with stories woven with evidence, creating a powerful pragmatic narrative. Ultimately, I was guided through positive self-reflection so that I could start to understand my ability to access Feminine and Masculine Energy in a synergistic fashion to enhance my health, personal relationships, and career success."

—**Tyler Maltman**, M.D. CCFP, Assistant Professor College of Medicine University of Saskatchewan

"In *Gender Physics*, Betty-Ann provides the right balance of personal experience examples, anecdotes, analogies, pointed research, and solutions to help women and men tap into both their Feminine and Masculine Energies beyond stereotypical gender expectations. Many of us working in industries dominated by the other gender will appreciate how she demonstrates that finding Feminine and Masculine Energy balance is a useful tool to achieve success in business, to be appreciated and recognized — even if at times the process can be scary or feel pretty foreign. Betty-Ann provides tactics to help us achieve balance so we may gain more confidence and experience increased fulfilment in all areas of life. Her insight allows the reader to explore their own biases, tendencies, and pulls and guides them to consider ways to avoid extremes and find the right equilibrium in their use of *Gender Physics* in everything they do and say. This is a must-read if you have ever wondered why your dominant go-to energy (whether Feminine or Masculine) doesn't always elicit the results you anticipated and how to improve your outcomes."

—**Véronique Loewen**, Communications Manager at Orano Canada Inc., and Owner Communicator, and Translator at Verolingo Communications

"In a world where we strive to find a competitive advantage, looking inward might be our best bet. Betty-Ann provides us with the tools to shift our energies in order to become dynamic, thriving individuals in both our personal and professional lives."

—**Dan MacIntyre**, Community Builder, Autoworker, Political Candidate

"Betty-Ann has done an incredible job in this book by turning her real-life experiences into examples of how you can integrate both Energies into your life for peak results. I would highly recommend this book to any forward-thinking female."

—**Mary Hipperson**, Commercial Sales and Leasing Agent, Concorde Group, Inc.

"Betty-Ann shows readers how to identify and engage one's internal Energies to reach their full potential. She honestly and effectively uses lessons from her professional career to illustrate the concept of *Gender Physics*, and then provides the tools to unleash and harness these Energies for success. The book is a must-read for young women starting their careers. No doubt with the knowledge of *Gender Physics* and these tools in hand, you will 'find your voice, take a risk, [and] stand your ground.'"

—**Mary M. Donlevy-Konkin**, Q.C., Senior Counsel, McKercher LLP